FINANCIAL DISCIPLINE ORGANIZATION

A Strategies Blueprint to Build Trustworthy, Resilient, and Future-Ready Organization

VENKATESH KAP

STARDOM BOOKS

www.StardomBooks.com

STARDOM BOOKS
112 Bordeaux Ct.
Coppell, TX 75019, USA

FIRST EDITION JUNE 2026

STARDOM BOOKS, LLC.
112 Bordeaux Ct. Coppell, TX 75019, USA

www.stardombooks.com

Stardom Books
United States and India

FINANCIAL DISCIPLINE ORGANIZATION

A Strategies Blueprint to Build Trustworthy, Resilient, and Future-Ready Organization

VENKATESH KAP

p. 298
cm. 13.97 X 21.59

Category : BUS041000 : BUSINESS & ECONOMICS / Corporate Finance / General
BUS027000 : BUSINESS & ECONOMICS / Financial Risk Management
BUS036000 : BUSINESS & ECONOMICS / Investments & Securities / General
BUS002010 : BUSINESS & ECONOMICS / Accounting / Financial

ISBN : 979-8-950206-01-6

DEDICATION

Dedicated to the Founders, CXOs, bankers - Borrowers, Investors-Investees, and financial professionals who work tirelessly to build trust, safeguard, and strengthen the foundations of our financial ecosystem.

ACKNOWLEDGMENTS

This book owes its existence to the many leaders who believe that financial discipline can transform lives and the economy. I am grateful to friends, mentors, industry practitioners, and learners whose questions, discussions, and experiences enriched the ideas presented here. Your insights shaped every chapter.

"In today's interconnected world economy, financial discipline has become the universal language of business success. This book is your foundational guide to mastering this critical skill set, designed for entrepreneurs, business leaders, and organizations across all continents, cultures, and commercial sectors. From emerging markets to established economies, from micro-enterprises to Fortune 500 companies—the journey toward financial excellence begins here."

CONTENTS

INTRODUCTION

Organizations that prioritize financial discipline do more than survive; they outperform. They grow with clarity, allocate capital with intent, and make decisions that hold steady across cycles. While others chase momentum, these companies build strength quietly. Their success is not accidental. It is designed through consistent choices, measured risk-taking, and a deep respect for capital.

Financial discipline enables growth that is sustainable, not fragile. It creates organizations that earn trust, attract better opportunities, and respond to uncertainty with confidence. Over time, this discipline compounds, turning stability into advantage and advantage into long-term value. This book is about understanding and building that edge.

Most companies don't go out of business because they have bad ideas, poor market potential, or lack ambition. Instead, they go out of business because they lose financial discipline over time as they achieve success and become more self-assured.

In fact, I have seen the same pattern recur across virtually all industries, businesses of all sizes, and all business cycles. Companies that possess robust product offerings are sometimes unable to sustain them; companies with strong and respected brands have been unable to hold them together; and companies that have talented employees and have had impressive growth have sometimes lost control over their organizations, even though it did not happen overnight; instead, it happened incrementally over a long period of time.

Although the warning signals are nearly always present, they are seldom taken seriously. This book focuses on that blind spot.

It has been some leaders who misunderstood that financial discipline means proper accounting. They often equate it with good accounting, clean audits, or frugal spending. Some see it as a temporary measure—tightening it during downturns and relaxing it during growth. Both views are incomplete. Financial discipline is not just a function, a policy, or a phase. It is an essential capability for the organization.

Financial discipline defines the frameworks for making decisions when real trade-offs exist. Financial Discipline shapes how we assess financial risk, allocate capital, transmit bad news, and establish accountability.

Financial Discipline determines whether growth contributes to or detracts from the organization, and, most importantly, whether success can be sustained or is fragile.

The rewarding speed, scale, and storytelling of the financial marketplace have made it accustomed to large amounts of available capital, high levels of risk tolerance, and overlooking the fact that many organizations view "discipline" as synonymous with "cautious". Today, the financial market has shifted. Volatility is back, capital is hard to find, and stakeholders (lenders, investors, regulators, and boards) now expect to see resilient operating models, not just growth.

This book presents an alternative way of thinking about finance – as a leadership function rather than a support function for operations. It challenges the belief that having clean financial statements equates with having control; that generating profit equates with security; and that meeting compliance requirements equates with having an effective corporate governance structure.

In its place, it promotes a Financial Discipline System that is purposefully designed, integrated into the organization, and practiced consistently across the entire organization.

You will be introduced to the concept of the Financial Discipline Organization (FDO), the FDO Framework, design the tools to assess and build financial discipline deliberately. This is not a theoretical exercise. It is a practical guide for founders, executives, board members, lenders, investors, and finance professionals who want to understand why organizations collapse and how some quietly endure.

Financial discipline does not make organizations slower. It makes them survivable. And in the long run, survivability is the most underrated competitive advantage of all.

This book brings together concepts drawn from real organizational contexts and lived financial experiences. While the principles of financial discipline are universal, their application will vary across industries, sizes, and stages of growth. Some ideas are illustrated through specific situations or types of organizations, not as limitations, but as anchors for clarity. The intent is not to prescribe a single approach, but to offer a way of thinking. Readers are encouraged to interpret and apply these concepts in ways that align with their own organizational realities.

1

THE HIDDEN THREAT WITHIN

Each day, most leaders spend much of their time focusing on the competition. Who will be the next new entrant to the market? Existing competitors' new product release, and who can innovate faster within that space?

But what happens if the actual "killer" is not an external threat, but rather, an internal issue within the organization that has crept in under the cover of short-term success and appears to be a strong performer relative to its competitors?

This internal killer is known as Financial Indiscipline. Financial indiscipline will never make the front page compared to other external threats, such as a competitor releasing a new product or a company being disrupted by external forces. Financial indiscipline does not knock at the door of your boardroom; it enters and takes root inside the organization through the innocuous accumulation of small choices and optimistic forecasts used to placate investors, such as taking out loans with no written plan on how to repay them, or utilizing excess budget within a department for unrelated expenditures that do not align with the organization's long-term objectives.

Although these choices may initially seem harmless and rationalized, if not addressed promptly, they accumulate and contribute to an ongoing culture of Financial Indiscipline, eroding your organization's resilience and building distrust among employees. Another example of Financial Indiscipline is the story of a well-known startup that the media celebrated for its rapid success and considered a unicorn due to its rapid growth.

Internally, however, it was burning through cash recklessly, enjoying lavish office interiors, incurring inflated hiring costs, and making acquisitions unrelated to its core business. Six months later, the same company that once graced magazine covers was unable to pay salaries on time. What outsiders saw as a sudden collapse was, in truth, the inevitable consequence of financial indiscipline that had been ignored for too long.

This is why financial indiscipline is a silent killer. It hides in plain sight, tolerated in the name of growth or strategy, until it suddenly manifests as a crisis. For leaders, the real question is not "Who is our biggest competitor?" but "Are we undermining ourselves from within?"

Defining Financial Indiscipline (FID)

Before they can confront a problem, leaders have to identify that problem. Many people equate Financial Indiscipline (FID) with a lack of proper accounting practices or poor financial management; however, FID is actually a more profound and more damaging issue.

FID does not stem from an employee's inability or failure to accurately report financial numbers. FID also does not exist only because of 'budget misallocations'.

FID is caused by a failure of leadership, which manifests in the way leaders and their organizations make decisions and take actions that ultimately punish their organizations and prevent them from establishing and maintaining sustainability. Think of it as the culture behind the numbers. Accounting is concerned with the record-keeping of transactions so that the financial books reflect reality. Financial Management's focus is on the allocation of resources, how and where to invest, and on optimizing returns on investment and growth funding. Financial Discipline is how leaders make decisions about those allocations, investments, and optimal growth funding in the first place. It is the invisible guideline for how leaders make their financial decisions that determines whether those decisions result in long-term viability and success, or produce adverse or catastrophic events that cause or contribute to the organization's downfall.

"Accounting records what has happened. Financial management allocates what is. But financial discipline shapes what will happen. Without it, even the best accounting practices cannot prevent failure."

When financial discipline is absent, organizations may still appear successful for a time. Revenues might grow, market share might expand, but the foundation is already cracking.

Type of Financial Indiscipline	Description
Poor Decision-Making	Taking loans or investments without visibility into repayment, expanding into non-core areas, or making risky investments without assessing downside risks. A promoter takes a massive loan for a new real estate venture while the core

	manufacturing business struggles. Initial optimism fades, and both ventures collapse.
Lack of Transparency	Management often misrepresents their company's cash flow as stable, even though they have short-term loans that they roll over every quarter. This is done to deceive stakeholders into believing they are in a better position. Once lenders discontinue extending credit, the company will collapse.
Mismanagement of Funds	Using the performing project/department cashflows to another new or non-performing project/department. The end use of the loan differs from its actual purpose. Frequently misuse statutory payments, such as provident fund deductions and GST collections, to cover non-statutory cash flow needs.
Unethical Practices	Manage EBITDA in the balance sheet. Some companies inflate the value of invoices they send to boost their group revenue on paper. While, at first glance, it may appear profitable from a financial perspective, it fails to produce actual cash inflows and therefore continues to bury them deeper in debt.
Conflicts of Interest	Inappropriately acquiring services from a family member-owned company or a closely-held family business. Additionally, it is inappropriate to enter into any transactions with closely held entities that erode value from all shareholders.

Case Study:

One of India's chemical companies was once a viable medium-sized entity. However, as a company, it regarded fiscal discretion, fiscal restraint, and cash management as something worse than nonessential.

Operations incur certain costs, which are reflected on the balance sheet (A/R, inventory), and obvious liquidity, which the company routinely mismanages. To create new businesses, the Directors made speculative investments. At the same time, they deferred payments to vendors to create cash for other, unrelated investments until they could no longer continue to do so.

The Directors also provided payment guarantees to vendors, but had no rules in place regarding how much or how quickly vendors would need to be paid. From the outside, it appeared to be a "pot o' gold" because revenue had a surprisingly steady range over time. But once cash was tight, the company collapsed under the weight of its own inadequacies. Vendors delivered no further products; lenders demanded repayment; the company filed for bankruptcy within three months of that date. The company's downfall was clearly attributable to poor management's "indiscipline," rather than to an unfortunate economic situation or a general lack of demand for its services.

This company did not collapse due to poor demand or adverse market conditions. It collapsed because leadership failed to exercise financial discipline.

Why Financial Indiscipline Is a Silent Killer

Financial mismanagement doesn't usually give you a wake-up call; instead, it creeps up on an organization. It begins with small things like seemingly innocuous or justifiable choices, like giving someone a loan "just this time" without evaluating revenue projections or exaggerating numbers to keep an investor happy.

By delaying two months' worth of vendor payments, all the little breaks taken out of necessity become habits. Therefore, you can see how financial mismanagement can be a "silent killer"; it hides behind positive financial statements, growing revenue lines, and successful trades and testimonials. As damage accumulates within an organization, it becomes unrecoverable.

Company X was a medium-sized organization that promised its investors double-digit annual growth. Still, it then made changes to its financial records to compensate for the lack of double-digit growth. Company X's board was happy with the decision, and it appeared to be going well to its investors; however, in reality, the Company was facing severe cash flow issues.

By the time lenders and vendors stopped providing credit, the gap between reported performance and cash liquidity was so vast that it was inevitable the business would collapse. To outsiders, the sudden collapse appeared sudden, but it was actually years in the making.

Examples of the failures of Satyam computers, Blockbuster, and Toys "R" Us demonstrate that corporate failure does not usually occur suddenly due to a decline in customer demand or poor products, but rather results from long-standing internal weaknesses related to discipline, leadership, and strategic judgment.

While Satyam Computers was ultimately undone by its long-term inability to maintain an accurate and truthful financial reporting structure, as well as its deliberate attempts to mislead its shareholders, customers, regulators, and employees through the manipulation of revenues and profits, the result of this deceit was the creation of an illusory stability and growth for the company.

Therefore, when the company's fraud was exposed in 2009, the years of trust built up in Satyam Computers were lost nearly overnight.

The reason Satyam Computers failed was not that it had inadequate demand for its products or that its technology was inferior, but rather that its financial numbers were fabricated. In contrast, Blockbuster's downfall stemmed from its inability to keep pace with strategic developments and adapt to changing times.

Where other companies were leveraging the advent of digital disruption, Blockbuster management chose to stick with the traditional DVD rental business model, while continuously and emphatically rejecting the idea that the emergence of streaming was a viable threat to its business. Blockbuster could have continued to offer customers the opportunity to rent DVDs. Still, Blockbuster management chose not to use the available tools to understand better how their customers consumed movies, and would like to do so. The failure of Blockbuster was not an unavoidable outcome but rather a failure to recognize the need for change and the discipline and foresight necessary to adapt as the movie market evolved.

After its leveraged buyout, Toys "R" Us incurred excessive debt stemming from poor financial management, which limited the company’s ability to invest in e-commerce and upgrade its operations, while competitors successfully capitalized on e-commerce.

Visible signs of financial stability were misleading and disguised the company's inability to adapt to changing market conditions; children have not stopped purchasing toys, but rather the inability to invest in e-commerce due to debt has resulted in a loss of strategic flexibility and an inability for management to innovate and reinvent the company until it was too late.

These cases exemplify that, in many cases, the decline of an organization is self-inflicted, resulting from a lack of integrity, rigid thinking, and financial decisions that make it impossible for the organization to continue adapting for sustainable success.

The Silent Killer Cycle

The accumulation of poor financial habits does not happen overnight. It does not come as a flash of insight in the form of one specific act that everyone will see.

Instead, the accumulation of these poor financial habits builds slowly through a pattern of seemingly small daily choices. Making a payment 30 days late or sending out slightly inflated cash flow projections can easily be justified as "temporary" or "necessary for growth."

Initially, these bad decisions do not threaten the business's future. Generally, these bad habits are often defended as practical. Business leaders often make statements such as "We'll fix this in the next quarter" or "This is just until our cash flow improves." Once the first breach of an acceptable business practice occurs, it opens the door to a similar, repeatable pattern. Over time, these patterns can become acceptable business practices that affect the organization's culture.

As such, financial indiscipline is often described as the "silent killer" of an organization; it sneaks up on the organization until it is too late to address the root of the problem, which has now become ingrained in the business.

By the time management recognizes the impact of financial indiscipline on the organization's financial structure, it will be too late, and the organization's actions will leave it unable to recover financially.

What outsiders see as a crisis event or failure is the culmination of years of business practices that have gone unaddressed and are unrealistic.

Financial indiscipline follows a predictable cycle:

The Cycle of Indiscipline

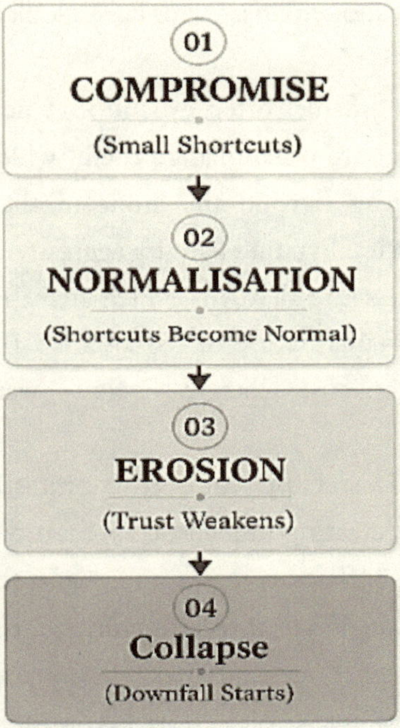

A cycle of financial indiscipline has destructive potential because it feels safe but is out of control and cannot be corrected after a company's collapse has occurred.

By the time Boards of Directors and investors recognize the risk, it is usually too late for a business to recover from its failure. The failure of most companies is not the result of a single mistake but rather of ongoing, uncorrected risks taken over time.

Organizations Do Not Have Financial Indiscipline Without Warning Signs

Leaders and boards usually ignore the signs of an impending collapse, even though these signs are usually visible for a long time.

They are commonly overlooked because of either being blinded by short-term success, which conceals the long-term risks, or by a justification by the board and/or management that they are employing "bold" strategies. Identifying these warning indicators shortly after they emerge can help management decide on timely corrective actions rather than incurring irreparable harm.

Categories of Indiscipline

There are several types of financial indiscipline. Let us have a look at them:

1. **Greed and Overexpansion:** Companies often expand into new product offerings or markets that are unfamiliar to them, which causes them to stretch themselves beyond the limits of their financial and managerial capabilities. Pyramid Saimira aggressively expanded its cinema screen business into all towns, which increased revenues; however, the unsustainable nature of its costs led the company's business model to collapse when cash flows were insufficient.
2. **Over-Optimistic Projections:** Leaders present overly optimistic projections to reassure investors, creating unrealistic expectations and pressure. Satyam Computers inflated revenues and profits for years to show unstoppable growth. When the truth emerged, the company collapsed almost instantly.
3. **Aggressive Spending and Diversions:** Cash is treated as limitless, lavish spending, premium offices, and unrelated acquisitions, thereby weakening financial discipline. Byju's spent heavily on premium offices, celebrity marketing, and multiple acquisitions unrelated to long-term sustainability, leading to a severe cash crunch and reputational fallout.
4. **Non-Core Diversions:** Companies drift from their core business into unrelated sectors, losing focus and burning capital. Ola diverted significant investments into electric vehicles and manufacturing without the needed scale or experience, weakening its core taxi-hailing business.
5. **Illegitimate / Political Money:** Accepting political or illegitimate funds creates hidden liabilities, governance distortions, and exposes the company to sudden regulatory or reputational shocks.

Why Leaders & Boards Miss Financial Irregularities

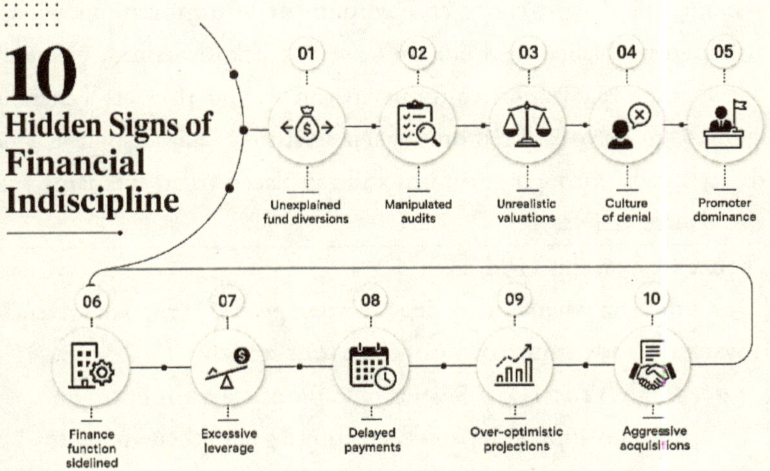

Many organizations tend to ignore financial irregularities and late reporting as long as they can get away with it. However, in practice, financial system failings and their promotional practices are typically not addressed until after the opportunity has passed.

The reason most leaders do not take action is that they are blind to their own practices due to entrenched systems of blind trust in the instincts of themselves and others in their network, or inner circle; lack of financial clarity among members of the board to challenge the story proposed by management; and lack of awareness among auditors as to the importance of culture to their professions, and consequently, validating numbers without questioning

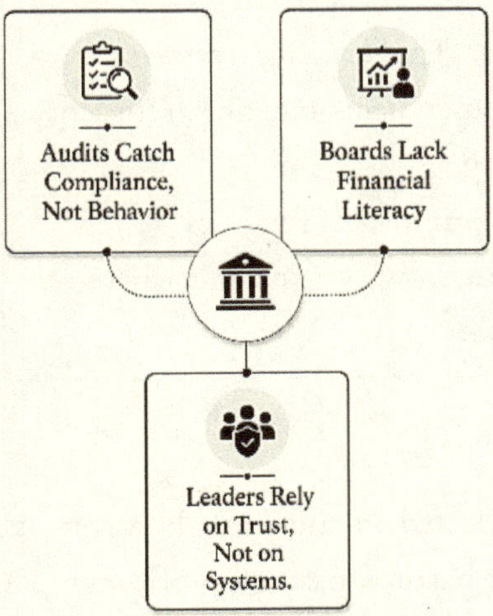

Why Governance Fails

the management behaviors that underlie them. All these forms of systemic blind trust create an environment in organizations where, although problems are seen, they are not acknowledged; elements within the organization continue to run it; and risks are generally ignored, to be considered only when a crisis is realized. By the time reality breaks through optimism and misplaced trust, the damage is already irreversible.

Trust vs. Systems Grid

Depending on whether they depend upon people (Trust) or systems (Systems), leaders fit into one of these four zones:

- **High Trust/Low System**: Decisions are made based on relationships with people, creating a gap in their ability to be disciplined.
- **Low Trust/Low System**: Complete chaos with no accountability or reliability.
- **Low Trust/High System**: The rules and systems, while rigid, create a safe environment that may come at the expense of flexibility.
- **High Trust/High System**: The ideal zone – Strong relationships supported by robust systems, resulting in efficient and disciplined decision-making.

The most significant number of examples of financial indiscipline occurs in the High Trust/Low System zone, where trust replaces checks and balances.

The Hidden Consequences

Financial indiscipline can be reflected in numbers; however, its effects extend beyond a company's balance sheet or profit and loss statement, with losses accruing beyond the company.

The condition may exist despite corporate profitability, but the damage resulting from financial indiscipline is already being felt by employees, vendors, investors, and the marketplace. More often than not, the "hidden" impacts of financial indiscipline are greater than any immediate impact on the profit and loss statement.

The repercussions of a company being financially undisciplined are not limited to collapse and include many negative aspects that arise long before a company goes out of business. One of the most damaging consequences of a company losing its credibility is that it no longer has opportunities to partner with other organizations. Trust has been lost, and banks are unwilling to lend because of a lack of confidence in the organization's financial position.

Likewise, many potential partners are unwilling to engage in business with other organizations for the same reason. When a company's business practices come into question, growth slows not because of a lack of demand or innovative ideas, but because the company has lost the trust of those who would otherwise be its customers or partners. In addition, declining employee morale is another visible consequence. Employees become aware of problems when their salaries are delayed or cut unexpectedly, or when they receive conflicting messages from management. All these inconsistencies contribute to a lack of confidence, which, in turn, increases employee turnover within an organization. For instance, a mid-sized company that is three months behind on its salary payments, but still presents itself as doing very well to investors. Employees who are aware of these discrepancies often leave the company before the collapse of that organization due to the lack of confidence they have in their management; losing experienced employees before a company's collapse has a weakening effect on that organization, especially at a time when it is struggling to find additional ways to grow.

Vendor mistrust arises when a company's finance department demonstrates poor control. Late payments or manipulating payment schedules erode a supplier's trust in a company. When this occurs, suppliers may shorten their credit terms, require payment in advance, or completely stop providing products or services to the company. Suppliers pulling back can greatly hinder operations because there is typically a ripple effect that slows them down and creates operational paralysis, increasing a company's financial strain.

Along with diminishing trust and slowing operations, poor financial management can quickly erode a company's good reputation.

Stakeholders start to think differently about a company, from being viewed as progressive to being irresponsible, or from being viewed as creative to being unreliable.

The years of hard work that went into building a company's good reputation may disappear in a matter of days when the company's financial misconduct becomes public. The markets, media, and business partners will quickly distance themselves from a company, making it challenging for the company to recover, even if it takes corrective actions later.

Clearly, financial indiscipline does not just affect the balance sheet; it also substantially undermines trust, morale, operations, and a company's overall reputation long before it officially fails.

How Indiscipline Cascades Across Stakeholders

Stakeholder	Trust Marker Lost	Long-Term Impact
Investors	Confidence in numbers	Withdrawal of funds, falling valuation
Employees	Assurance of stability	Attrition of top talent, morale collapse

Suppliers	Payment reliability	Halted supply, stricter terms, legal disputes
Customers	Product/service continuity	Switching to competitors, loss of market share
Regulators	Compliance and governance	Investigations, penalties, restrictions on growth

Enron, Wirecard, WeWork, and Theranos are examples of organizations that once reached great heights and received widespread praise and admiration; however, they were quickly brought down by hidden manipulation, a toxic corporate culture, and a lack of self-discipline.

The demise of one of the SME companies was a direct outcome of years of financial deception through hidden financial statements (using off-balance sheet financing) by way of manipulative accounting, a culture of toxic behaviors in which employees were encouraged to cheat and steal, and a culture in which these SME employees were expected to produce inflated revenue numbers or face termination. This SME's demise led to an enormous loss of employee pensions, ruined countless careers in the financial services profession, and irreparably damaged the public's environmental perception of corporate governance.

Similarly, one of the Mid-Corporate has experienced an ongoing series of fraudulent activities (e.g., hidden financial statements, false representations in audits, inflated cash position, etc.) that have led to the exposure of these activities and a significant decline in investor and regulatory trust. This Mid-Corporate's rapid decline highlights how fragile a company's credibility becomes after an organization loses its integrity, particularly in the financial services sector, where confidence and oversight are essential.

One of the large corporate financial collapses may have occurred at a different time than many of the other companies included in this book, but, like other failures, it is rooted in a lack of discipline. Its valuation was based primarily on hype rather than on sustainable financial performance, while the leadership team took excessive risk and failed to implement basic financial controls.

This behavior led to an investor exit, widespread employee disillusionment, and a loss of faith among many landlords, partners, and stakeholders, even after a significant effort to stabilize and implement a recovery plan; nonetheless, it has caused significant long-term damage to this large corporate brand and its credibility.

One of the enterprises is an extreme example of deliberate secrecy and inflated expectations. The company knowingly presented falsified test results as if they were developed with a revolutionary new technology that did not exist. A government-ordered investigation quickly took place, and the company was ultimately closed down, and the executives were made to answer for their actions.

This Enterprise scandal resulted in the complete collapse of trust (from investors, patients, and the general public). The findings of the analysis of these business cases illustrate a critical fact about ambitious companies that achieve short-term success through deception or illusion. If companies have ambition without integrity and discipline, they have the potential to cause catastrophic damage to a large number of individuals, businesses, and institutions, regardless of the company's size.

Financial indiscipline is never confined to the finance department. It spreads into lost opportunities, weakened morale, broken supplier relationships, and destroyed reputations. By the time the balance sheet reflects the damage, the organization is already in decline.

Case Study: Collapse & Recovery

The ups and downs of companies that were once celebrated illustrate the problems of financial indiscipline. Those stories - of collapse and recovery - illustrate that decision-making by leaders, rather than just the market, is one factor in determining whether a company survives.

Collapse Cases			
Company	**Core Cause of Indiscipline**	**What Happened**	**Outcome**
Kingfisher Airlines	Indiscriminate borrowing, unchecked expansion, and inability to manage liabilities	Borrowed heavily to finance expansion; failed to pay salaries; suppliers withdrew support as debt ballooned.	Shut down in 2012 due to mounting liabilities despite a strong brand image.
Lehman Brothers	Excessive leverage, hidden risk exposures, and short-term profit chasing	Took on massive leveraged positions and concealed risks; vulnerable when the 2008 crisis hit	The collapse triggered a global financial meltdown, systemic failure due to financial management
Carillion	Aggressive contracts, poor liquidity management, and a lack of risk controls	Pursued large projects without financial safeguards; debts rose; projects failed.	Imploded in 2018; employees, suppliers, and taxpayers absorbed the fallout.

Recovery Case			
Company	**Crisis Situation**	**Actions Taken (Discipline Restored)**	**Outcome**
Chrysler	Bankruptcy was caused by high debt levels, declining demand, and poor efficiency, culminating in the 2008 crisis.	This resulted in divesting non- core assets, incurring restructuring costs, securing government support, tightening governance procedures, aligning spending with strategy, and introducing/enforcing risk controls.	Emerged leaner, profitable, and stable, demonstrating that discipline enables recovery

Indiscipline versus Discipline in Action		
Decision	**Financial Impact**	**Root Cause**
Lavish expansion & unpaid liabilities (Kingfisher)	Debt spiral, loss of supplier trust, collapse	Leadership ego, lack of cash discipline
Excessive leverage & hidden risk (Lehman Brothers)	Triggered the global financial crisis, bank implosion	Greed, short-termism
Reckless contracts & debt (Carillion)	Supplier defaults, employee losses, total collapse	Mismanagement, lack of oversight
Asset monetization & core focus (Chrysler)	Debt reduction, operational stabilization, and regained trust	Governance discipline, cultural reset

Diagnosing Early Warning Signs

To identify early indicators of financial malpractice, you must go beyond just analyzing reports. It's easy to change how some data looks. A company's audited financial statements may provide a false sense of security, as its auditor may not see or report all material concerns.

Therefore, the company's leaders/board should look for minor, but significant, warning signs.

What Checks Miss	
Audits Check	**Audits Miss**
Compliance with accounting standards	Leadership intent and behavior
Accuracy of recorded transactions	Cultural patterns of indiscipline
Conformance to disclosure rules	Early warning signs of liquidity stress
Internal control processes	Normalization of compromises within the organization

Every year, the board of a company received "clean" audit reports, yet the company was internally experiencing deteriorating cash flow and rolling over short-term loans quarterly. Although the board received comfort through the audit sign-off, they were shocked to find layoffs and vendor defaults due to a liquidity crisis.

Compliance has been verified through an audit, but it does not reflect an organization's overall culture. Rather than relying solely on the audit report, Boards and Investors should question both the Company and themselves about identifying potential Red Flags that are not disclosed in the Financial Statements.

The cost of not maintaining Financial Discipline is much greater than simply losing a few numbers.

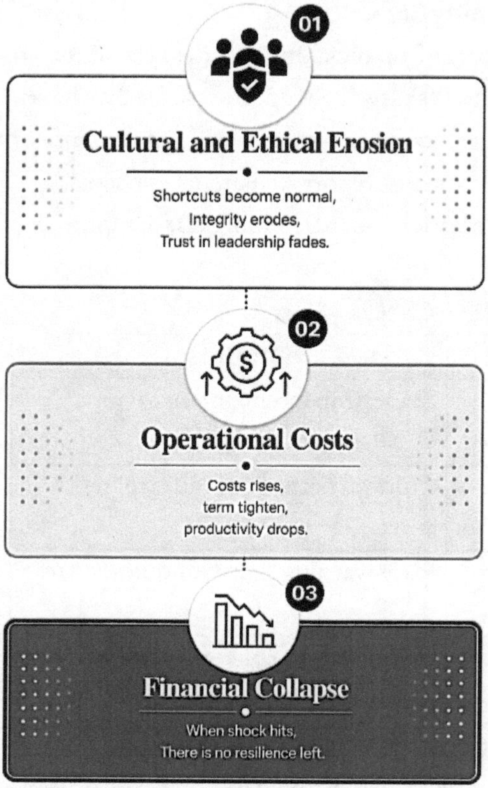

When Investors lose confidence in their company, their customers lose trust, Suppliers discontinue support, Employees lose morale, and the Community loses trust as well. Each Stakeholder pays a price for a Leader's failure to act on early signs of issues. By allowing the harm to go on without any action, a Leader is left unable to fix the damage.

Ignoring financial indiscipline is doing nothing; it is a refusal to face the problem. Failure to address this matter will erode the organizational culture, increase the costs of doing business, and hasten the organization's demise due to financial insolvency. The next chapter will outline the outcomes of an organization that chooses not to confront the effects of financial indiscipline and will explain how such a failure occurs at the systemic level rather than as an isolated incident.

At its core, financial discipline is not a technical matter; it is a leadership competency. Leaders are often measured by their vision, strategy, and ability to execute. However, without disciplined financial management, even the most innovative vision will fail.

Leadership Impact = (Vision × Strategy × Execution) × Financial Discipline.

While the vision gives direction, the strategy outlines a timeline for accomplishing it. Finally, execution yields positive outcomes if done correctly.

Financial discipline ensures that whatever the results are, they are dependent upon your approach towards capital; therefore, the ability to maintain your company's financial health during both a strong and weak economy is primarily determined by your level of discipline. Your vision may be perfect, but without discipline, your chances of success are minimal. However, when your focus/vision is narrow, yet your discipline is outstanding, your long-term outcome will reflect your generosity to others.

The CEO was required to make difficult decisions about his company's expansion strategy due to an impending recession.

He and his team would take a conservative approach, focusing on liquidity and long-term viability rather than risking their financial well-being. As a result, when the economy turned, the CEO's organization not only survived the downturn but also grew even more successfully than before. Other businesses took huge risks, but the majority either couldn't survive or failed.

Culture and vision are both critical; however, without adequate financing and financial discipline, they cannot survive.

Financial discipline is a necessity, not an option; it determines whether executives make decisions about their organizations that build resilience or cause them to fail. Founders, investors, and board members all assess their effectiveness as stewards, in large part, by the extent to which they incorporate financial discipline into all financial decisions, contractual agreements, and strategic growth planning activities.

2

THE COST OF NEGLECT

Storytelling is common in every business. A precarious one is, "For now, we'll concentrate on expanding the company, and later, we'll address company discipline."

At first, this statement seems okay. It starts with a few payment delays; the company provides overstated financial projections; and the company allows expenses to be approved, even though the return on investment is not adequately analyzed, and the founders rationalize each expense as temporary. What the founders may regard as temporary decisions are seen by the board members as an appropriate approach to growth. Investors also accept these short-term decisions for the sake of growth. What begins as a temporary trade-off soon becomes normalized into corporate culture.

The simple truth is that financial discipline is not a choice a leader or executive can turn on or off as the company expands. Once indiscipline has ingrained itself, it creates a hurricane of adverse effects on the organization, trust, and systems, which no longer have the structure to support a return to success.

The Decline of Financial Responsibility

Neglect is predictable; once it starts, you set a trajectory toward disregard for all aspects of your business's financial dealings. Small compromises may seem reasonable, such as delaying payments to suppliers, miscalculating projected liabilities, or overstating potential growth. Over time, these only grow larger and larger, and the business becomes increasingly negligent of its financial obligations because the entrepreneurial type of freedom seems to justify these behaviors. As it continues down this road, the business will soon be in a position of what is called a "financial death spiral.

The Four Phases of Financial Indiscipline		
Phase	**Name**	**Description**
1	**Compromise**	Under pressure, leaders begin to relax standards, making minor exceptions that weaken discipline.
2	**Rationalization**	Human beings need internal narratives that support their bad choices, so that we see every compromise as either a strategic decision or a necessary one.
3	**Normalization**	The stakeholder group has stopped questioning individuals' behavior; therefore, reduced discipline has become part of the institutional culture on a daily basis.
4	**Collapse**	Economic hardship, the downturn in the economy, a regulatory investigation, and the scrutiny of professionally sanctioned investors manifest as a system collapse. The collapse happens quickly but is not created overnight. Instead, it is built.

At every stage, leaders convince themselves that the damage is temporary. But the spiral is not temporary. It compounds.

"Financial losses show up in quarters. Trust erosion shows up in decades."

Why Leaders Miss It

Neglect is a slow-motion tragedy because it happens without a sense of danger, even as companies appear to be succeeding, raising funds, and growing market share. It takes time for an organization's indiscipline to become apparent to its insiders. Leaders often fail to recognize that eroding trust with employees, investors, and vendors will come at an incredible cost in credibility. If any of these groups come to question management's word, the process of rebuilding that lost credibility will take years rather than merely quarters. What is at stake for these organizations is not just a financial statement; they're playing with their license to operate. Leaders sometimes think they're using that lack of trust as leverage; in reality, they're wasting one of the most precious commodities available: trust, which is compounding exponentially faster than monetary investment.

Visible and Invisible Losses

When organizations talk about financial wellness, they re mainly discussing things that can & are measured like Revenue, Margin, Debt Ratio, and Cash Burn (The visible portion of the iceberg). Many discussions take place within board meetings & investors regarding these metrics as they are easy to quantify.

While the metrics listed above are critical components of a business's Financial Health, the most dangerous aspect of an organization lies beneath the surface:

The Invisible Losses (where organizations typically fail) are much more challenging to measure than the visible metrics; however, their effects can be much more damaging: erosion of trust, decay of culture, broken partnerships, and damage to Reputation.

Leaders who only track visible losses do not understand how compounding impacts the invisible losses. An overdue invoice is not simply a liquidity issue; it also represents a lack of reliability to the vendors. Inflated projections represent accounting treatment rather than confidence in the company. Every invisible "crack" weakens what may ultimately lead to collapse.

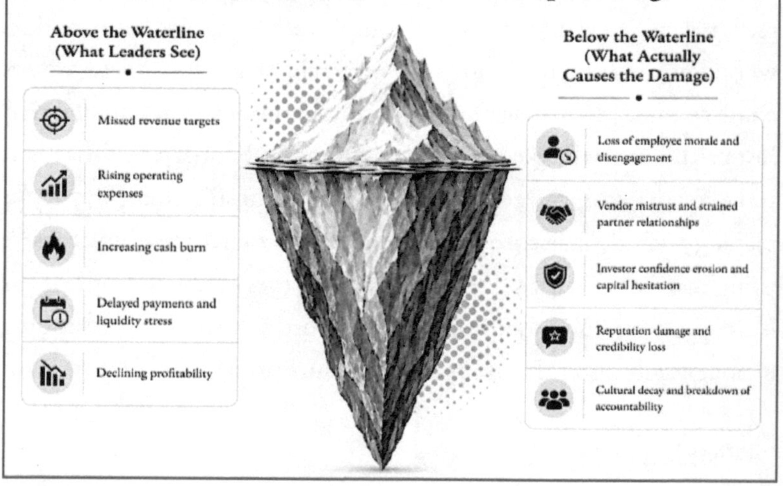

The Iceberg Model of Financial Discipline Neglect

An organization announced 20% revenue growth over three consecutive quarters. The board was congratulatory toward the management team, and investors began doubling their investments. However, what went unnoticed by the board and investors was that vendor trust had deteriorated.

Vendors are now experiencing frequent delays and are only willing to do business with companies that pay in advance for raw materials.

As for revenue, this organization continues to grow. However, from a working capital standpoint, this organization is experiencing a steep decline; its operational efficiency is decreasing rapidly, and its credibility is quickly disappearing. The organization was declared insolvent six months later, not due to a lack of customers, but instead to a lack of belief in what they were saying within their ecosystem.

Leaders typically place too much weight on financial figures while underestimating the importance of trust in their decisions and actions; this approach too often leads to destruction within an organization—not necessarily as indicated by what appears on the balance sheet but through damage that goes unaccounted for and continues to build until it causes more extensive losses throughout the organization.

Stakeholder Fallout

Financial neglect creates a ripple effect beyond just the accounting department, affecting all stakeholders (founders, employees, investors, lenders, vendors, consumers). Each stakeholder faces erosion of trust at different rates, with a common outflow of consequences once faith in the organization is lost; these typically occur very rapidly and often cannot be reversed.

Every stakeholder associated with an organization is affected by financial misconduct, typically in predictable yet terrible ways. However, the timing of the signs may differ across groups; the totality of the impact creates a crisis that, by necessity, contributes to an organization's ultimate demise. One group who suffers most significantly from financial misconduct is founders; in many instances, a founder has made considerable sacrifices before a company's formation, and as such, the line between the founder's professional accountability and their personal accountability becomes extremely blurred. Oftentimes, a founder must collateralize their personal assets and rely on personal guarantees when securing financing to maintain the business; over time, this can only go so far in mitigating poor business practices, as demonstrated by the downfall of Kingfisher Airlines. As Kingfisher Airlines' debt increased, its founder, Vijay Mallya, continued to back/evolve his personal endorsement (as collateral) to obtain loans.

Ultimately, Mallya's personal endorsements were of no consequence during the airline's demise; when Kingfisher Airlines failed, it led to the demise of Mallya's business and his personal reputation as well. The overall lesson: a founder's credibility does not replace effective internal control of an organization; therefore, in instances of failure, founders will typically lose the company, their wealth, and their good name.

Employees typically identify financial difficulties early on. The combination of late payments, frozen benefits, inconsistent communication from management, and untrustworthy reassurances leads to a breakdown in employee trust. As trust diminishes, productivity declines until the most productive employees depart, creating further internal weaknesses. Jet Airways suffered similar problems due to regular payment delays, resulting in a loss of both talent and service quality. Customers observed reduced service and consequently stopped purchasing tickets, further exacerbating the airline's woes. Re-establishing trust with employees after it has been broken can be extremely difficult, resulting in the loss not only of personnel but also of their ideas, creativity, commitment, and exceptional service. Investors and lenders will react quickly when they observe signs of financial mismanagement or a lack of clarity regarding an organization's finances. Investors and lenders no longer have faith in a company that cannot meet its contractual obligations or provide clear information about its financial performance.

As a result, capital will be withdrawn at the first signs of doubt, frequently before the general public is even aware of the situation. For example, during the collapse of Lehman Brothers in 2008, once investors lost faith in the organization's financial position, they quickly withdrew their funding, leading to its collapse.

It's important to note two key lessons from this. First, money leaves a company much faster than it enters, and second, investors and lenders rarely re-establish trust in an organization once it has been lost. Often, vendor and partner relationships respond more quickly than investors. Vendors will often take a tactical position by reducing or changing their terms of trade, asking for advance payments on their supplies, and withdrawing any support, if possible (or altogether). This creates short-term operational paralysis and may disrupt supply chains that support the affected business's operations. One of the mid-size companies, despite announcing a $480 million partnership, was under cash pressure, prompting vendors to request up-front payment for their supplies. As a result, they experienced a large number of employee resignations, which led to the breakdown of their partnership within 90 days. Vendors seek reliability, and when a vendor's reliability is questioned, the resulting "cascading failures" can doom long-term strategic relationships.

Although customers respond much more slowly than vendors, when a customer leaves a retailer or supplier relationship, it's one of the most final exits a business can experience. Once the quality of service, the delivery of goods, and the supplier or retailer's financial stability decline in the customer's eyes, there's virtually no chance they will return to the business. Blockbuster provides the perfect example of this: Blockbuster's declining service and Netflix's much better customer service created an opportunity for customers to leave Blockbuster and migrate quietly to Netflix.

Eventually, the cumulative effect of those quiet movements of Blockbuster customers paved the way for Blockbuster's rapid demise. Trust once lost is often invisible at first; however, the damage caused is often permanent.

When combined, these examples illustrate how a business's actions surrounding financial discipline ultimately not only negatively affect the business itself but also erode the trust of all stakeholders in that company, thereby creating a "cascading failure" that becomes more difficult to recover from as it gains momentum.

Stakeholder Fallout Map			
Stakeholder	**Trust Lost**	**Long-Term Impact**	**Example**
Founders	Personal credibility	Loss of control, burnout	Kingfisher Airlines
Employees	Morale	Attrition, productivity decline	Jet Airways
Investors & Lenders	Confidence	Withdrawal of funds, tighter terms	Lehman Brothers
Vendors & Partners	Payment reliability	Supply halted, partnerships destroyed	Data Stream; Carillion
Customers	Faithfulness	Market share loss, which means competitor advantage	Blockbuster

Founders experience personal ruin, employees become disengaged, investors abandon the organization, vendors tighten their terms, and customers defect to the competition when financial neglect begins to impact stakeholders rather than just the organization. Eventually, the organization will become so hollowed out that it cannot continue operating even if demand for its products or services remains.

Thus, it is clear that financial indiscipline can no longer be considered purely the individual mistake of the organization's owner/founder; it is a systemic issue that is likely to take down everyone connected to the organization.

The Fall from Grace of Founders

As organizations begin to spiral into a culture of financial indiscipline, a founder may believe that, with sheer willpower and determination, they can keep everything together.

They will convince themselves, and then convince their creditors that they will delay them until the next month, convince employees that everything is okay, and instill hope and optimism in their investors and the public. In essence, a founder presents an image of control and solidity. However, even though they may present themselves as strong and stable, the pressure of their financial situation is having a dramatic effect on their personal psyche and emotional state.

Neuroscience explains this. Under conditions of chronic financial stress, the brain's decision-making centers narrow their focus to only the short-term, immediate challenges of survival. All thoughts regarding long-term strategy become inconsequential. Creativity decreases, sound judgment becomes scarce, and leaders who were once strategic in their decision-making processes become reactive and emotional. Purchases of time are less about being resilient and more about extending survival just long enough to secure enough financing to continue existing.

It should be noted that this downward spiral does not occur overnight. The downward spiral occurs gradually over a 12- to 18-month period, until the organization reaches a point of no return.

Over a period of about a year, the process of financial mismanagement usually goes through a series of stages, beginning with someone being unaware of their financial situation and ending with total financial collapse.

The decline may be subtle. However, as the company progresses through each phase, it gradually loses control, grows increasingly stressed, and becomes less trustworthy, making it difficult to reverse the downward trend.

The first few months of the downward trend will typically reveal some very early signs of financial difficulties. During this period, some late payments are made, and delays in the company's financial reporting are increasing. In addition, small mistakes in day-to-day operations will continue to occur more frequently. Although the company is experiencing financial difficulties, the founder will usually exhibit confidence and control over the situation. The founder will reassure employees, vendors, and investors that the situation will improve as the company grows. The founder may rationalize these early signs of trouble as "temporary" or "strategic" in nature. At this point, the owner continues to maintain a high level of control and believes they can fix the situation.

During the next three months (months four to six), the early warning signs continue to intensify, yet the founder continues to ignore them. The founder's ongoing optimism is based on future projections that predict a turnaround "next quarter. As a result of these mounting financial problems, the founder is forced to take out emergency loans, often secured by the founder's personal guarantee. While the company can still operate and deliver services, the founder's fear of what might happen if the company fails is outweighed by hope and the belief that it will succeed. At this point, the owner is losing significant control over the company and relying more heavily on personal credibility rather than making the necessary changes to address their financial problems.

As we look at months seven through nine, the pressure builds, and the mask comes off. Vendors begin requesting payment in advance, indicating a lack of confidence in the company. Employees are talking to each other about the lack of timely or no paychecks. Employee morale is declining. Investors are asking for clarity and transparency, but the founder spends more time managing their image than resolving the issues at hand. Quick fixes arise, and strategy quickly vanishes as the founder loses control of their business and their ability to provide leadership. The founder reacts to demands rather than strategically leading their company, and their focus is off as the quick fixes make the long-term effects much worse.

The last few months ultimately resulted in the total collapse of the facade that had been created. Creditors are unwilling to provide additional credit, investors stop providing additional funds, and a large number of employees leave due to a lack of trust in the company's management. The visionary founder is no longer a visionary—they are merely seen as unreliable. Compromise becomes the norm, and the company thrashes and founders without any support. Control is less than ten percent, trust is gone, and failure is inevitable.

This twelve-month period is a perfect example of how financial irresponsibility typically does not lead to a dramatic outcome. Instead, it erodes control, confidence, and effective leadership gradually, until there is nothing left to support the company.

A founder of a consumer company delayed rent for the company while reassuring investors that the company is on track to expand and grow. The landlord calls every day looking for rent, and the vendors require payment in advance. However, during board meetings, the founder presented/created flashy presentations and gave aggressive targets. While the illusion was being maintained, it worked until vendors stopped delivering product, and employees started missing their paychecks. At this point, investors were able to see through the optimistic veneer due to the liquidity crisis. Investors were too late to realize that the optimist was hiding the financial weaknesses of their business, and therefore, the founder's credibility diminished within weeks. The founder's background provides insight into why financial discipline is a human problem rather than a numerical one. Leaders under pressure do not suddenly suffer catastrophic failures; instead, they experience minor, incremental breakdowns that lead to a gradual loss of control. Once the actual demise occurs, the leadership cannot recover because it is unable to act.

Case Studies

❖ IL&FS

Infrastructure Leasing & Financial Services (IL&FS) was once a symbol of trust in India's infrastructure sector. With over 300 subsidiaries and associates, it was deeply intertwined with banks, mutual funds, insurers, and governments. For decades, its reputation masked its weaknesses. IL&FS's poor governance allowed it to borrow heavily with no real control over those borrowings. There was also a significant delay in project cash flows relative to scheduled repayments, and defaulted loans have been disguised through the issuance of additional loans. Despite indications of financial trouble and continued confirmation of financial integrity by auditors and rating agencies, the organization was headed for failure. The failure of IL&FS unfolded quickly: 2018 - Numerous warnings of project delays were generated. Mid-Year 2018 - Failure to meet interest payments raises concern within the financial sector. September 2018 - IL&FS defaults on repayments, triggering panic among banks, mutual funds, and insurance companies.

Aftermath: Infrastructure projects across India stall; banks freeze lending; mutual funds face redemption pressure. The systemic nature of IL&FS meant its failure was not just corporate, it was national in scope. Hundreds of projects were delayed, investors lost billions, and the government had to step in with emergency measures. IL&FS demonstrated that when a central financial institution practices indiscipline, the ecosystem collapses with it.

❖ Carillion

Carillion, a UK construction and outsourcing giant, followed a disturbingly similar trajectory. For years, it won major government contracts despite a balance sheet weighed down by debt. Payment terms to suppliers were stretched further and further, effectively making small contractors bear the brunt of Carillion's financing needs.

As in the case of IL&FS, oversight failed. The auditors endorsed the accounts. The government continued issuing contracts to Carillion, and vendors continued to provide supplies in anticipation of receiving payments. The collapse happened quickly and devastatingly:

1. **2016:** Carillion aggressively pursued new contracts, despite operating on slim profit margins.
2. **2017:** Company debt was growing quickly, but dividends were still being paid to show that the business was viable.
3. **January 2018:** Carillion entered insolvency with £7B in liabilities. After the collapse, over 30,000 suppliers and subcontractors went unpaid, construction at many hospitals and schools was halted, and many people lost their jobs and pensions.

Carillion exposed how a single contractor's indiscipline can devastate an entire ecosystem. The collapse eroded confidence in public-private partnerships across the UK.

Ecosystem Ripple Map		
Layer	**Impact of Indiscipline**	**Long-Term Effect**
Core Company	Defaults, project delays	Loss of credibility
Partners & Vendors	Unpaid dues, contracts delayed	Bankruptcies, supply chain collapse
Investors & Lenders	Value writes down, credit frozen	Withdrawal of capital, higher risk premiums
Communities& Governments	Stalled projects, abandoned services	Public damage distrust, socioeconomic

"Financial recklessness destroys strategic partnerships permanently and cannot be repaired."

Organizations have the ability to mend their own financial records; however, ecological systems do not have that option available to them; therefore, whenever Suppliers, Investors and Governments lose faith/trust in an ecosystem, they will always apply permanent punishment through tighter regulations, higher costs and less frequent interaction, as well as creating a very stringent regulatory environment that will limit the total number of customers and communities served by that ecosystem. The results of IL&FS and Carillion illustrate that once a business has destroyed or lost the ecosystem's trust, that ecosystem will no longer be able to sustain the organization, even after it has recovered financially.

The tables and explanations below are designed for Entrepreneurs, Administrative Professionals, and Regulatory Authorities to quickly, efficiently, and effectively identify issues before they become major problems or crises.

Description	Purpose	What It Reveals	Key Warning Signal
Iceberg of Neglect	Shows visible vs. invisible financial damage	Cultural decay, trust loss, and reputation risks	When visible numbers look fine, but internal cracks grow
Productivity Destruction Formula	Measures how indiscipline impacts performance	Leadership time drain, stagnation, and firefighting	When leaders spend more time fixing today than planning tomorrow
Vendor Trust Factor	Captures early signs of external distrust	Vendor behavior, payment credibility, supply risk	Vendors switching to advance-only terms
Early Warning Checklist	Practical diagnostic for boards + regulators	Behavioral and operational red flags	Multiple indicators occurring simultaneously

The Iceberg of Neglect				
Layer	**Description**	**What Leaders Usually See**	**What They Miss**	**Example**
Visible Losses (20%)	Tangible, measurable performance impacts	Missed targets, cash burn, delayed projects	Accurate scale of underlying instability	Revenue growth hides internal resignation and delayed payments

Invisible Losses (80%)	Cultural and trust- based deterioration	Not reflected in P&L or audits	Morale collapse, vendor mistrust, reputation decay	IT services firm: staff attrition + vendor advance-only terms despite revenue growth

Productivity Destruction Formula				
Stage	**Organizational Reality**	**Leadership Focus**	**Productivity Level**	**Illustration**
Healthy Discipline	Strategy-driven, predictable operations	Growth, customers, innovation	~100%	Leadership meetings centered on expansion
Early Neglect	Cash flow issues start consuming attention	Balancing short- term fires	~60–80%	Increasing talk about collections, delayed payments
Severe Indiscipline	Firefighting dominates leadership time	Crisis response, placating stakeholders	~0–20%	70% of weekly meetings focused on cash survival

Vendor Trust Factor			
Driver	**Explanation**	**Trust Movement**	**Example**
Consistency (Years of reliability)	Long-term on-time payments	Trust builds slowly	Vendors extend credit easily
Time (Single delay)	One delayed or missed payment	Trust collapses instantly	Fuel vendor refuses credit after a short delay
Vendor Trust	Trust =	Inverse	Advance-only

Factor Formula	Consistency ÷ Time	relationship	terms activate immediately
Impact	Supply chain freezes, operations stall	Organization enters survival mode	Airline collapses within 6 months

Early Warning Checklist		
Indicator	**What It Means**	**Why It Matters**
Finance team excluded from decisions.	Decisions made on intuition or authority	Early sign of structural indiscipline
Forecasts repeatedly pushed to "next quarter."	Over-optimistic assumptions	Reality is being denied, not addressed
Vendors shifting to advance-only terms.	Vendors have detected weakness	Supply chain stress begins here
Leaders avoid lenders, auditors, or investors.	Fear of scrutiny	Information asymmetry is widening
Clean audits but cultural red flags	Behavioral failure masked as compliance	Audits detect the past, not intent

The explanations above have also shown us the productivity theory, vendor trust factors, and an early-warning checklist available to every board and regulatory body as tools, not just theoretical guidance; with these explanations, boards can evaluate their commercial activity.

They are similar to how physicians assess their patients' health through routine (baseline) evaluations before ordering more specific testing and procedures.

When applied early, these assessments can indicate cracks in the structure before complete collapse; however, when applied after the fact, they can only serve as forensic tools to investigate the reasons for the collapse(s).

The Case of Neglect

Byju's was a widely recognized e-learning business in India that exemplified this progression throughout its existence. Byju's began their journey with an insatiable need for financial success and status. The company demonstrated significant instability in terms of how it managed financial records and made financial decisions, which eventually resulted in failed business operations, loss of investor confidence, multiple laws being broken, multiple unfortunate business deals going negative, and finally resulting in mass layoffs, fleeing investors, and the investigation and financial collapse of the company. Byju's was not destroyed by weak demand for education. It was undone by its own failure to embed financial discipline.

The collapse happens over time as a direct result of leaders ignoring early warning signs (i.e., through neglect).

By doing so, they are not just taking on more risk than they need to; they are, in fact, creating a surefire path to failure.

When a leader neglects financial discipline, their organization will collapse at some point; the 'when' is really just a matter of time.

Financial indiscipline is not just a possibility; it is something that happens to an organization. It starts small and grows into something enormous because of the leader's actions. When leaders fail to provide discipline to their organization, they place not only their organization but also all the employees, investors, suppliers, and the entire community at risk when the organization ultimately collapses.

The actual cost of neglect is not measured in balance sheets. It is measured in broken partnerships, destroyed livelihoods, and lost public trust. That is why financial discipline must be treated not as a technical function, but as a leadership responsibility.

3

WHY FINANCIAL DISCIPLINE IS NOT JUST ACCOUNTING

The financial statements presented by a founder in a boardroom were perfectly accurate and printed in perfect order. They were compiled from audited, reconciled, and certified without exception. Everybody present at the meeting was very relieved that the management team had received so much faith from their investors and performed with such quiet pride when describing the business's financial position or success. Everything appeared to be completely compliant with the best standards of corporate governance.

However, the same report did not disclose the fact that the business was burning through cash at an unsustainable rate. All of the vendors had begun to withdraw their credit lines from the business, some employees had begun to comment on delays in reimbursing expenses, and the company's commitment to expansion far exceeded the available cash on hand. Approximately nine months after being "in good standing" about the financial condition of the business, the same company found itself fighting for its life.

I learned the hard way that clean accounting does not equal financial discipline. It is possible to organize numbers to demonstrate order amid chaos or to indicate a level of health for a business on the brink of failure. Clean accounting is essential for maintaining a healthy financial position, but it cannot do so on its own.

Financial reports can be thought of as "backward-looking". They contain precise representations of an organization's past performance, but they do not guarantee future performance or protect against future performance issues.

Similarly, an income statement may reflect a company's current profitability but may fail to reflect structural weaknesses that will lead to its eventual failure.

A critical risk that leaders face is to mistake the fact that financial reports are precise as an indication of the organization's financial discipline. It is easy to assume that since the financial reports are accurate, the organization must be financially healthy.

In fact, accounting allows organizations to report what has taken place, but it does not establish the integrity of their choices. Financial discipline encompasses the leadership, mindset, and culture that support or hinder decision-making, helping prevent poor financial decisions from arising in the first place.

In this chapter, we explain the distinctions between financial reporting and financial discipline. If you believe that hiring a qualified accountant or preparing accurate audits and reports means that your organization has sufficient financial discipline, you are operating in a high-risk environment.

Financial discipline is not about how well your records are maintained; it's about the strength of your past decisions.

Financial discipline determines whether an organization will prevail after a financial shock or will be unable to withstand it.

Bookkeeping, Reporting, and Discipline

I've often observed in executive meeting rooms that leaders usually seem to stumble over the meanings of "accounting", "finance", and "discipline". These meetings often do not result in mortal consequences, but they represent inherent risk when one defines technical accuracy vs. the ability to execute strategic decisions. To support leaders effectively and diligently, we need to understand the three major components of Financial Intelligence: Bookkeeping, Reporting, and Discipline. Each of these is critical, and the large majority of failures related to Financial Intelligence can be attributed to leaders confusing one component with another.

The Three Layers of Financial Intelligence

1. **Bookkeeping**: Recording transactions. Accuracy and compliance.
2. **Reporting**: Interpreting records. Understanding past performance.
3. **Discipline**: Governing decisions. Shaping the future.

When these three are aligned, organizations are resilient. When they are not, collapse becomes inevitable.

Consider a SaaS company.

- Bookkeeping ensures that every subscription is recorded correctly.
- Reporting aggregates those records into monthly recurring revenue, churn rate, and gross margins.
- Discipline goes further: it evaluates whether the customer acquisition cost is sustainable in relation to the lifetime value of a subscriber. A company can report substantial MRR and low churn while still destroying value if the cost of acquiring those customers far exceeds their contribution.

This is why discipline must take precedence over reporting. It is the governing lens that tests whether apparent growth is real growth. Even the most skilled accountant cannot solve inherently strategic problems:

1. **Resource allocation:** deciding where money should be spent to maximize long-term resilience.
2. **Cultural mindset:** building an organization where financial prudence is respected, not sidelined.
3. **Risk appetite:** defining how much risk the organization can realistically bear.

An accountant can faithfully record and report. But without leadership discipline, those reports may document the company's journey toward collapse.

While both financial discipline and accounting are interrelated, each serves a different purpose: Financial discipline provides the basis upon which businesses operate, while accounting provides an overview of what has happened historically; whereas accounting gives the business a look at its current state of financial health, financial discipline focuses on how to continue operating in a disciplined manner.

As an example, many leaders confuse the importance of clean audit reports with the need for clear evidence of financial discipline. By confusing these two items, business leaders often overlook a greater truth: their organization is deteriorating from within.

The Illusion of Clean Books

The idea that having clean books automatically means having a disciplined approach to managing their financial operation has become one of the most significant pitfalls business leaders fall into today. I have witnessed many business leaders announce publicly that their financial accounts are reconciled, their audits are unqualified, and they meet all compliance requirements. Yet none of this offers assurance that their company will survive in the long term. Just because a business has clean numbers does not mean the company was disciplined in its decision-making process when spending the money reflected in those clean numbers. The purpose of accounting is to verify and reconcile the accuracy of the recorded costs incurred and revenue earned, as well as the timely filing of any federal and state tax payments. However, accounting does not provide insight into whether those funds were used wisely, whether risk was appropriately managed, or whether the company's growth was built on a sound foundation. Although clean numbers may be accurate, they are meaningless to a company's success if they result from undisciplined decision- making.

What Clean Books Show	What They Hide
Every marketing expense is recorded under the right head	Whether the marketing spend generates positive unit economics
Salaries are accounted for in the payroll ledger	Whether the team structure is bloated or sustainable
Loans and interest are reported correctly.	Whether the borrowing was prudent or reckless
Revenue recognized per accounting standards	Whether the revenue is repeatable or not
Compliance with accounting norms	Whether the company is building resilience for shocks

The Marketing Spend Illusion

Consider the example of a company that approved a multi-crore marketing budget. Every invoice was booked correctly, every vendor payment made on time, and every report tied neatly to the accounts. Everything appeared to be in order from an accounting perspective.

However, unit economics told a different story. The cost of acquiring each customer was double the lifetime value that the customer would bring. Growth was accelerating, but value was being destroyed. The accounts were clean; the strategy was reckless. Within two years, the company faced a liquidity crisis that no amount of accounting accuracy could prevent. The Chief Financial Officer (CFO) is known for his attention to detail and precision. Every line item in the company's financial statements was reconciled daily; all external audits of the company could be completed with almost no questions raised by the auditors; and the company presented to its Board of Directors in a very efficient and orderly manner. The investors had great respect for the discipline applied in financial reporting. When the economic situation changed, however, the company was not ready for it. Cash flow dried up, lending standards tightened, and the CFO had no means to assess future risk.

While he was able to trace the company's financial resources to their use, he could not provide a reasonable explanation for how, when, or where the company would obtain more. Less than two years after this event, the company was no longer in business because its leadership had confused compliance with proper discipline.

I have identified three symptoms of the **Clean Book Syndrome**:

- Overemphasizing compliance: If the auditors have signed off on the financial statements, the company must be sound.
- Reactive decision-making: The company provided accurate historical financial information, but had no plan for the future.
- Risk aversion masquerading as carefulness: Fear of making bold statements, such as "Should we expand?" or "Can we afford it?" led to a preference for keeping things tidy by producing only accurate records.

- The syndrome is seductive because it provides leaders with a false sense of control. A company can look perfect in the rear-view mirror while heading straight toward a cliff.

While having Clean Books (financial records in order) is essential, they do not guarantee clean record- keeping. A Clean Book does not prevent leaders from being undisciplined. Leaders may have clean records, but if they lack a disciplined approach to decision-making, they may realize too late that accuracy does not equal sound judgment.

Leadership Versus Financial Discipline in Real Financial Decision-Making.

The primary demonstration of quality in Financial Discipline does not lie in the books. It lies in how leaders create and execute decisions using the financial records. To that end, discipline dictates what action to take relative to how you arrived at your decision, and there can be a critical difference between resilience and failure.

1. Leadership uses financial accounting to conduct business based on financial records. To that end, discipline dictates how your organization uses the accounting function to make sound business decisions.
2. Leadership does not assess how much money it has spent based on its financial records; Leadership assesses what product or service it obtained from the expenditures.
3. One assesses the transaction; the other assesses the outcome. This concept helps demarcate between organizations that merely maintain Books and those that create enduring value.

The Courage to Say No

I once provided advice to a firm that had secured a significant contract worth ₹150 crores. From an accounting lens, this contract appeared attractive. Its revenue looked reasonable relative to costs, and it had an adequate profit margin. However, through the disciplined lens, the entire contract presented significant underlying risks. To deliver this contract, the company would need to expand its core competencies. The company would ultimately have to eliminate critical teams to use debt-funded working capital for the project.

In other words, the contract was technically profitable but strategically destructive. Leadership had the discipline to say no. That decision preserved the company's focus and liquidity, enabling it to win two sustainable contracts later.

Financial discipline is not simply the pursuit of every opportunity that presents itself; it requires you to be strategic and discerning. It is about choosing strength over vanity.

The more profitable 'no' is often worth more than the reckless 'yes.' WeWork's plunge can be viewed on the international stage as a typical example of aggressive masquerading as ambition. They aggressively expanded their options by acquiring businesses unrelated to their business model. Every acquisition was documented in the books and appropriately reported, but there was no clear strategy guiding the acquisitions. And once capital dried up, the acquisitions were like liabilities that exacerbated the fall. General Electric provides a more sobering example. GE has acquired businesses across various industries, including finance and entertainment.

The accounting had always been complete and meticulous, but eventually the diverging strategic fit built up, creating an obfuscation that accounting could not overcome. What began as diversification decayed to dilution.

In either event, they demonstrate a reality: unblemished records of bad decisions are still records of bad decisions.

How can leaders distinguish between accounting neatness and disciplined judgment? A financially disciplined leader consistently demonstrates these behaviors:

1. **Aligns decisions with long-term strategy** rather than short-term revenue.
2. **Tests risk appetite honestly,** asking what the organization can afford to lose, not just what it hopes to gain.
3. **Interrogates unit economics to ensure** growth is profitable at the customer level.
4. **Protects liquidity,** refusing opportunities that compromise the company's ability to withstand shocks.
5. **Involves finance early,** not as a reporting function after decisions are made.
6. **Prioritizes transparency,** ensuring the board and investors see the real trade-offs behind decisions.

This checklist is straightforward, but it distinguishes leaders who use numbers as justification from those who use discipline as a governance tool.

The Profitable No Culture

In most organizations, leaders celebrate success when they take advantage of significant opportunities; however, very few organizations celebrate the insight it takes to say "no" in a disciplined manner, and financial discipline appears to be the opposite of "spending" money.

For example, saying no to over-expanding your company, to making reckless acquisitions, and to borrowing money at unsustainable interest rates are all acts of maturity that preserve your company's resources, help you focus on your company's core business, and create relationship-building opportunities with your stakeholders.

Unfortunately, the accounting function can't capture this cultural aspect of saying no to make the right decision for an organization; instead, it only captures revenue lost or not recognized because the organization couldn't prevent the right decision from taking place.

Time and time again, organizations that foster a culture of saying no have demonstrated their ability to outperform organizations that chase any opportunity that comes along.

The bottom line is clear: accounting will tell you whether you recorded an event, but discipline will tell you if you are making decisions that will serve your organization in the future.

Numbers tell you what happened in the past; however, only discipline can help us prepare for the future.

The Qualities of a Financially Disciplined Organization

Financially responsible organizations are unique and set apart from their financially irresponsible peers, not necessarily by the accuracy of their accounting systems, but by the culture of discipline they create.

Financial Discipline Organizations (FDOs) work proactively to anticipate, prepare for, and manage their financial performance, and therefore can consistently operate with financial prudence rather than reacting to crises when they occur or when auditors uncover issues.

In my experience, three primary characteristics define financially disciplined organizations. They have a focus on *capital intelligence in the future, a culture of intelligent restraint, and a distributed form of financial ownership.* A disciplined financial organization is based on a set of principles that define how its leaders view capital, risk, and long-term decision-making.

The principles are not solely based on the idea that growth or profit generation should be the only focus. Instead, they also emphasize resilience, intentionality, and shared responsibility across the organization.

Future-oriented capital intelligence is the first of these principles. Although capital is typically viewed as a tool for generating profit or facilitating growth, disciplined leaders see it as a strategic weapon; therefore, they are entirely focused on achieving liquidity through stress testing and modeling worst-case scenarios and opportunity costs before capital is used. When discussing capital and how best to use it, leaders should focus less on headline revenue numbers and more on cash runway, downside protection, and contingency planning. By employing future-oriented thinking, organizations can remain prosperous during economic downturns, generate excess profits through opportunistic investments when competitors operate at reduced capacity, and maintain a high level of strategic flexibility over the long term.

Another defining principle is an intelligent culture of saying "no". Disciplined organizations do not view the refusal of high-risk or low-value opportunities as a sign of uncertainty, but rather as a sign of strength.

Leadership will reject deals, acquisitions, or expansions that take the focus away from what is essential, add an unmanageable amount of debt, and serve vanity and not strategy. By refusing to take an opportunity that is not in the organization's best interest, the organization protects itself from costly mistakes and builds credibility with investors, vendors, and employees. Over time, the discipline of saying "no" will build trust and demonstrate that long-term stability is more important than short-term excitement.

The proper integration of financial stewardship into every decision an organization makes is effective. Financial discipline is not only the Finance Team's function. Sales teams analyze the impact of credit terms on cash flow; Operations consider inventory to maximize dollar use; and Management assesses the financial implications of committing people, time, and capital to new initiatives. Once financial stewardship permeates all of a company's functions, that discipline becomes entrenched in the organization's culture. Therefore, daily decisions by all employees align with the organization's overall financial health, enabling it to preempt potential crises before they materialize.

Together, these create organizations that are not only financially sound but also strategically durable, capable of navigating uncertainty, resisting unnecessary risk, and sustaining long-term value. For many years, I have dealt with a manufacturing organization that, despite enjoying consistent revenue increases, continued to suffer cash flow issues, mainly due to "control issues" within finance departments. The CEO's immediate response was to pressure the CFO to obtain additional debt finance. We worked together to create cultural shifts in how financial responsibilities are distributed across all departments, thereby fostering shared accountability for financial management.

As an example, procurement began using standardized procedures to negotiate tighter credit terms through vendor contracts. Sales leaders began aligning customer contracts with customers' payment timeliness, or "payment behavior"—operations consolidated operations to reduce the amount of idle money tied up in inventory.

As a result of these actions, the amount of working capital required was reduced by approximately 30% in less than 18 months, allowing additional cash to be spent elsewhere and enabling the organization to operate without additional finance costs.

The point I make when discussing this situation is that developing financial discipline is not only the responsibility of the finance department; it is primarily a cultural issue. Once an organization's culture shifts towards a collectively responsible, disciplined finance culture, it becomes more resilient. Therefore, the key to maintaining financial discipline is for executives to focus on building a culture of accountability, foresight, and restraint within the organization. These three specific qualities will separate organizations that will survive through difficult times from those that will collapse during their initial challenge.

Systems and Audit ERP

Often, when speaking with company executives or management about the company's financial controls, one will hear, "We have an ERP in place; our books are audited; everything is under control." This is a very positive response to receive from your leadership team, and it is easy to understand why the executives and managers feel confident; however, that confidence is often misplaced. Although systems and audits are necessary, they are not substitutes for discipline. They can create a false sense of security, preventing executives from realizing there may be larger challenges to face.

The ERP Illusion

ERP (Enterprise Resource Planning) systems are excellent at integrating data; however, if an organization's culture is weak, ERP becomes an effective way to present an image of what the systems do rather than what they do not. An ERP represents a paradox: "garbage in" results in "gospel out." Subsequently, when a number is entered into the ERP, it is accepted as accurate, and when management or auditors review it, it is accepted as valid.

If the number was originally bloated or inaccurate, the ERP will merely magnify the inflated value.

Even though auditors play an important role, that role is limited because they only ensure that a company complies with an accounting standard and do not provide assurance to the user of the financial statements as to whether the financial statements reflect a sustainable model for generating revenues. For example, if an audit is to assure whether revenue recognition complies, the audit would not assure that the revenue model will result in sustainable cash flow over time. Similarly, while an audit may verify that expenses are recorded to the correct account, it does not assure that the expenses were reasonable in the circumstances.

While a clean audit will identify irregularities, it cannot determine whether a company has good habits or employs preventive measures to avoid financial difficulties. I had recently reviewed the expense processes of a company. I found that every employee's travel expenses had been recorded accurately in the ERP, and the system could indicate who approved the expenses, reconcile receipts to expenses, and locate items that did not match.

The ERP system appeared to work well in theory; however, upon evaluating the underlying substance of what was occurring, we determined that there was significant abuse at the expense-reporting level.

For instance, some employees had been inflating their mileage claims, splitting hotel bills, and booking refundable tickets that they canceled after receiving reimbursement for the purchase. The ERP system was not designed to monitor an employee's intent to commit fraud, so it was unaware of fraudulent activity; therefore, the company was celebrating compliance while losing money.

ERP / Audits Provide	Financial Discipline Demands
Accurate recording of transactions	Judgments about whether spending creates value
Verification of compliance with standards	Alignment of spending with strategy
Assurance of historical accuracy	Foresight about future resilience
Detection of anomalies	Governance of choices before they are made
Clean reports and dashboards	Culture that resists manipulation

While systems have tremendous capabilities, they cannot find reason. They process information that leaders put into them. Similarly, an audit can find mistakes but cannot stop bad behavior. ERP connects several areas of a company, but does not foster a culture of honesty.

Financial discipline must be part of a company's leadership to be effective, and it cannot be outsourced or treated as a machine problem. Discipline should guide the system, not the system determining how disciplined we are.

Auditors and ERPs may show that the numbers are correct; however, they do not create healthy organizations. Only leaders' decisions create true resilience in an organization and its systems.

From Accounting Function to FDO

In view of all of this, for many organizations, Finance starts as a fact-based practice that tracks transaction and institutional flows, produces Financial Statements, and facilitates Regularity. While this is undoubtedly important for organizations to perform, it is only the first stage of their journey. As an organization matures, developing Financial Discipline into an Organizational Habit requires it to go beyond being fact-based and to develop Financial Discipline within the organization. Therefore, I have named this development of Organizational Financial Discipline the FDO Bridge Model. The model outlines how an organization can achieve success through:

1. **The Technical Layer**: That layer that keeps track of Financial Transactions and Financial Reporting, maintains Financial Independence, and assures all laws and practices are being respected.
2. **The Strategic Layer**: Using Historical (Financial) Data with Financial Modeling to assist in Making Decisions, Evaluating Potential Capital Deployment relative to risk appetite, Conducting Liquidity Stress Tests, and evaluating the Possible Impact of Opportunity Cost.
3. **The Cultural Layer**: Developing a Culture of Courage to continue developing Financial Discipline as a Routine in the Day-to-Day Lives of Employees, where the responsibility of managing corporate finances is not just the CFO, but is embedded in all members of the organization.

An organization becomes a Financial Discipline Organization (FDO) only when it crosses all three layers. Clean books are the foundation, but culture is the capstone.

Translating Jargon into Business Impact

Language poses some barriers in these situations because Finance uses technical terminology that some leaders don't understand, which can feel separate from their day-to-day efforts.

Therefore, Discipline needs to communicate the impacts of its uses in business rather than just providing simple definitions.

1. Variance should not be considered a financial term. It refers to the performance gap between the commitment made and the results delivered.

2. An accrual is not merely a financial accounting technicality; it reflects the timing disparities that exist within a company. In certain situations, these timing differences can directly affect liquidity, jeopardizing a company's ability to continue operating.
3. Working capital is not a ratio. It is the freedom to run the business without constantly taking on debt.

When finance speaks the language of business impact, it ceases to be a department and becomes a decision-making partner.

Accounting Mindset to FDO Culture

1. **Accounting Mindset**: "Are the numbers correct?"
2. **Strategic Finance**: "What do these numbers mean for our decisions?"
3. **FDO Culture**: "Are our behaviors creating resilience?"

This progression reflects the shift from compliance to strategy to identity.

Accounting View and Discipline View in Key Business Decisions			
Decision Area	**Accounting View**	**Discipline View**	**Key Outcome**
Expansion Choice	Chooses the lowest upfront cost	Considers long-term demand, strategy, and scalability	Lowest cost is not always the best choice
Vendor Selection	Picks the cheapest bid	Prioritizes reliability, quality, and long-term value	Total value outweighs price.
Sales Credit Terms	Records revenue at the sale	Assesses cash flow and payment risk	Better cash discipline improves stability
Acquisitions	Focuses on deal feasibility	Evaluates strategic fit and long-term impact	Feasible does not mean wise

Frequent accolades of compliance, as if compliance were an accomplishment, are common among companies. Having a clean audit, on-time reporting, and accurate reconciled ledgers are necessary; however, they do not constitute sufficient reason for a celebration of sorts. Companies should only celebrate when financial discipline creates overall value. This means good financial discipline within teams can provide them with reduced working capital, increased liquidity, or protection against risk.

An example of how a company created this cultural transformation was by encouraging operations to work with Finance rather than just auditing. Incentives were given to sales leaders to decrease the timeframes for customers to pay invoices.

Incentives were awarded to operations leaders for reducing inventories that were unused or idle. Within two years, profitability rose by 30%, not due to changes in how the accounting team performed its functions, but to the creation of an environment in which financial discipline was valued and respected.

Its systems or its reports do not define an FDO. It is defined by the way people think. When managers pause to ask, "Does this decision build resilience?" before signing contracts or approving projects, discipline has crossed the bridge from a function to a culture.

This is the shift every organization must strive for: from compliance to value creation celebration. Only then can finance move from being a department to being an identity.

Cultural Shifts and Financial Discipline Identity

The final stage of financial discipline is cultural, where discipline is no longer an activity managed by finance but an identity embraced by the organization. In such companies, discipline is not something people *do*; it is who they *are*.

Financial discipline is typically restricted to the finance department within many organizations. Decisions made by departments other than finance are often made without regard to finance, with finance brought in afterward to reconcile. This organizational structure does not work well under any scenario; it is very flimsy and vulnerable. Financial discipline as a role is easy to bypass; however, when financial discipline becomes an identity for employees, they cannot disregard it.

In an FDO, employees are recognized for who they are and what they can do by making decisions in a disciplined manner. A sales employee is respected for their ability to close a deal, but also for negotiating deals that contribute to profit margins and maintain cash flow for the organization. An operations leader is valued for running a manufacturing operation efficiently, but also for helping the organization to maintain appropriate levels of working capital. Even entry-level employees should be able to answer the question, 'Will this expense result in a benefit to the organization?'

One of the many salespeople at her company was extremely successful and changed the way contracts were set up. She knew instinctively how terms of payment, discounts to be provided, and service obligations could affect profit over time.

By negotiating better credit terms and avoiding offering discounts that could not be sustained, she protected both margins and cash flow. Her impact was greater than that of a large number of financial statements because she did this at the moment a decision was made.

She showed that financial discipline is not merely a designation; it is an approach every employee can take to fortify all positions within the organization.

The Transition of Identification

The most flexible firms do not ask if their financials are balanced; they ask if their staff are consistently financially conscientious. If all personnel are held to be disciplined in financial matters, financial discipline is a component of the organization's brand.

Investors seek it, partners appreciate it, and competitors respect it.

In terms of identity, this shift from compliance to a competitive edge removes the need for companies that implement a culture of financial discipline to fear going out of business; they have developed a reputation whereby they have a positive image in the marketplace, a positive image will attract new capital and talent, and provide new opportunities. Accounting is necessary but it is not a complete solution; balance sheets and timely audit findings provide order, but do not create resilience. Financial discipline is more than an accounting function of the past; it is establishing financial discipline in the future. This provides an overall leadership perspective, establishes a corporate culture, and supports the development of future-oriented strategies within an organization.

The distinction between progress and process is essential because some businesses mistakenly equate the two.

The lesson learned is obvious: process does not equate to progress, and accounting accuracy does not protect a company against indiscipline. A foundation is needed for any building, and the pinnacle of a structure gives it function.

The most significant potential for fiscal stability is established at the top of the hierarchy. Therefore, while it is essential to obtain statistical data on one's financial health, it does not necessarily mean one is financially well off; similarly, taking a diagnostic medical test does not guarantee one is physically fit. Ultimately, the road to health stems from a disciplined lifestyle and doesn't rely solely on statistical data.

4

WHAT IS A FINANCIAL DISCIPLINE ORGANIZATION (FDO)

A fortress may not look glamorous, but it endures the storm. Consider two companies I encountered simultaneously in the same market.

Company A appeared to be the darling of the ecosystem. Its branding was stylish, its offices were impressive, and all the business outlets were covering its fundraising rounds. The founder was charismatic, investors were lining up for oversubscribed rounds, and employees were receiving extravagant perks. A glance at the surface, and Company A looked like a success.

Then, the market changed. A funding environment that turned south, combined with operational inefficiencies, exposed what was beneath the glitter. The company was burning cash in an unsustainable manner, it was trapped in expensive commitments, and it was plagued by financial indiscipline. Within eighteen months, it folded. Vendors stopped supplying, employees scattered, and investor support stopped.

The end was not a surprise; it was the predictable outcome of an organization built around image and indulgence, rather than discipline.

In contrast, Company B received little press. It had modest offices and a leadership team that seldom, if ever, spoke at conferences. Internally, however, it was operated with an uncanny degree of rigor. Decisions were made with financial discipline. Growth occurred at a steady rate rather than erratically. Reserves were created in a disciplined manner, cash flow was managed with discipline, and expansion was considered only if it aligned with and created long-term robustness. When the same downturn arose, Company B reduced discretionary spending, communicated transparently with stakeholders, and honored its obligations. They survived the turmoil and garnered market share as weaker players lost their competitive advantage and folded.

The difference between the two companies was not branding, sector, or even profitability. It was designed. Company A depended on good times; Company B was prepared for bad ones. Company A had a finance department; Company B was a Financial Discipline Organization.

This is the central thesis of this chapter: a Financial Discipline Organization (FDO) is not a company that looks strong from the outside, but one that is resilient from the inside. It is not defined by fundraising success or glossy reporting. It is defined by governance, culture, systems, and leadership aligned to create long-term value.

FDOs are not loud, but they are durable. They do not mistake appearances for strength. They know that financial discipline is not a department or a function—it is a mindset, a backbone, and a way of operating. The strongest organizations are not always the most visible. They are the ones with fortresses built of discipline.

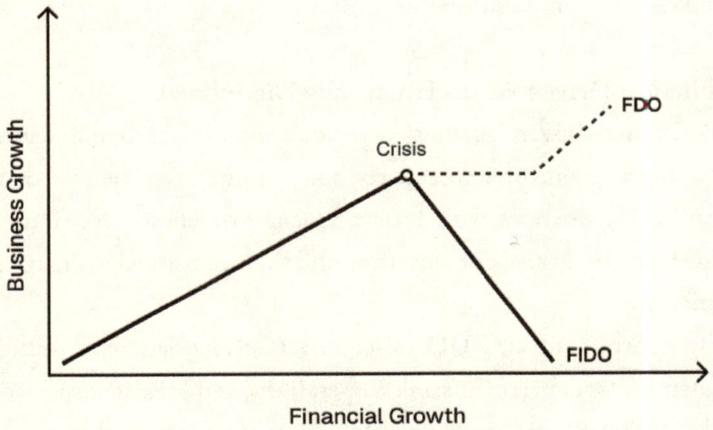

In a nutshell, how Financial Discipline Organization (FDO) and Financial Indiscipline Organization(FIDO) perform when a crisis arises

Defining a Financial Discipline Organization (FDO)

Some companies believe they are financially disciplined simply because they have a functioning finance department. Salaries are processed, accounts reconciled, and audits completed on time. But financial discipline is not about operational neatness. It is about resilience by design. A Financial Discipline Organization (FDO) is one where governance, culture, systems, and leadership align to embed discipline across all levels of decision-making. It is not a function; it is a mindset and infrastructure that shape how an organization behaves in both good and bad times.

An FDO is not defined by size, profitability, or sector. A small business can operate with more discipline than a billion-dollar corporation. Similarly, a profitable company can still be fragile if its discipline is absent.

What distinguishes an FDO is intent: the conscious decision to build resilience, not rely on momentum.

Finance-Driven versus Financially Disciplined

A **finance-driven business** depends heavily on its finance team to clean up, explain, or retroactively adjust numbers. The rest of the organization operates with little financial awareness. Decisions are made based on instinct or ambition, and finance is asked to "make the numbers work."

By contrast, in an **FDO**, discipline is everyone's responsibility. Leaders across departments, sales, operations, and HR, are expected to make decisions that strengthen the company's financial backbone. Finance does not fix after the fact; it partners in decision-making upfront.

Financially Lucky versus Financially Disciplined

Some companies appear resilient simply because conditions have favored them. A booming market, easy credit, or a sudden spike in demand can mask indiscipline. These are the firms I call "financially lucky." They mistake temporary fortune for strength.

FDOs, on the other hand, prepare for volatility. They conserve cash, stress-test strategies, and create buffers before a crisis arrives. When the environment shifts, luck-based firms collapse while FDOs survive and often emerge stronger.

Finance Department–Centric Business	Financial Discipline Organization (FDO)
Finance is seen as a support function	Finance embedded as a leadership mindset
Clean books and audits are the goal	Resilience and sustainability are the goals

Finance "fixes" decisions after they are made	Finance shapes decisions before they are made
Success depends on favorable conditions.	Success is designed to withstand volatility.
Discipline is episodic (during audits, crises)	Discipline is continuous and cultural

The lesson is clear: financial discipline is not a department, nor is it a matter of luck. It is a deliberate design that integrates governance, culture, systems, and leadership into one resilient fabric. In the following sections, we will unpack the **core discipline** of an FDO and explore how organizations can embed discipline so profoundly that it becomes an integral part of their identity, not just a checklist, but a way of life.

The Core Disciplines of a Financial Discipline Organization

A Financial Discipline Organization is not an accident. It is the result of deliberate choices that embed discipline into how the organization governs itself, allocates capital, manages risk, and responds under pressure. These disciplines are not policies or frameworks layered on top of the business—they are operating realities that determine how decisions are made when conditions are uncertain or hostile. At the heart of every FDO are five core disciplines. Each is essential on its own, but their real strength lies in how they reinforce one another. When these disciplines operate together, they create an organization that is difficult to destabilize—even when markets turn, leadership changes, or growth accelerates.

Core Disciplines of a Financial Discipline Organization (FDO)			
Discipline Area	**What It Means in Practice**	**Behavior in an FDO**	**Observed Outcome**
Governance	Strong, independent oversight	Clear approval rights; board-level challenge	Preserved liquidity
Financial Strategy	Purpose-led use of capital	Rejection of vanity growth and cosmetic metrics	Sustainable growth
Transparency	Honest and timely reporting	Regular cash reviews; early warning signals	High stakeholder trust
Risk Management	Anticipation over reaction	Scenario planning; liquidity buffers	Crisis resilience
Resource Allocation	Capacity-aware investing	Disciplined cost and investment decisions	Durable performance

These disciplines do not function in isolation. Governance establishes accountability and prevents drift. Financial strategy ensures capital is deployed with intent, not optimism. Transparency enables early course correction rather than late-stage firefighting. Risk management fosters preparedness rather than dependence on heroics. Resource allocation protects long-term capacity rather than chasing short-term appearance.

When these disciplines are embedded, the organization gains something that cannot be engineered through surface-level controls: structural resilience. It may not always appear aggressive or flashy, but it remains steady when others are forced into reactive decisions.

What distinguishes a Financial Discipline Organization is not how impressive it looks in good times, but how reliably it holds together when conditions deteriorate.

How FDOs Behave in Times of Stress

Every company looks confident in growth markets. The real test of resilience comes when conditions tighten—when funding slows, demand contracts, or shocks ripple through the system. It is in these moments that the difference between appearances and discipline becomes stark.

In terms of cash strategy and cash management behaviors, a "flashy" or non-disciplined organization views cash as fuel. It grows quickly by hiring people, occupying more office space, and creating new brands, assuming the continual availability of capital. A financially disciplined organization (FDO), on the other hand, views cash as oxygen; it manages cash by establishing and preserving liquidity buffers, aligning operating expenses with predictable revenues, and eliminating wasteful discretionary spending.

With this disciplined approach, an FDO can continue to operate fully even during times of cash constraints.

When an FDO faces a cash constraint, decision-making under stress reveals the disparity between financially disciplined organizations and flashy, or non-disciplined, organizations. Flashy organizations, being penny-wise and pound-foolish, strive to maintain a high profile, attempt to create a false sense of confidence for investors by continuing to spend heavily on promotional activities, and promote a "growth-at-any-cost" philosophy. FDO focuses first and foremost on the organization's survival and runway; they halt all non-core initiatives, re-negotiate their operating costs, and methodically slow their growth rate, extending their working capital runway to protect their core business and maximize the potential for recovery when economic conditions improve.

Market downturns highlight the different-similar responses. In many cases, companies that lack financial discipline will respond to downturns with denial and delays. These companies continue to grow even though they have received many clear warnings that bad things are going to happen, believing instead that the downturns will soon reverse. FDOs, on the other hand, will pull in early and purposefully-they begin pulling in their resources back to core business activities and focusing on achieving financial resilience. This allows FDOs to create a lean, financially stronger organization that will be primed and ready to capture market share when the economy begins its rebound.

In addition, under the stress of market downturns, organizations exhibit very different communication patterns with their stakeholders. Companies that are undisciplined in their financial management typically provide selective disclosures about the current state of the company, focusing on good news or optimism, without considering the potential ramifications of current conditions. Financially disciplined companies will be open, frequent, and fact-based in their communications with the boards of directors, creditors, employees, and customers. This level of transparency preserves stakeholders' trust and increases their willingness to support the company during difficult periods.

Finally, the relationships developed with creditors and investors can demonstrate an organization's financial discipline. Companies that create flashy images will often communicate only when they absolutely need to. The results of these delayed communications can create surprise and severe credibility damage when an organization experiences an issue. In contrast, FDOs will communicate proactively and transparently. They will share actual cash balances and describe the corrective actions they are taking early and often.

This proactive communication preserves access to capital and creates an opportunity for organizations to have a breathing space during stressful times.

Taken together, these behaviors show that under pressure, financial discipline is not simply about being austere; it is also about creating clarity and credibility and enduring long enough to recover from a downturn.

The difference between the two companies I watched unfold in parallel illustrates this point.

A **flashy startup**, backed by prominent investors, collapsed within a year of funding drying up. Its leadership had built a cost structure that assumed infinite capital. When the downturn hit, they scrambled with last-minute layoffs and desperate fundraising pitches. Partners cut ties, employees left, and the collapse was swift.

A **conscientious mid-size** company operating in this sector acted differently. It had accumulated cash reserves during years of growth, pursued long-term, profitable projects, and built a culture that rewarded prudence. When the recession hit, it reduced discretionary expenditures, maintained open communication with stakeholders, and paid its debts. Not only did it survive, but it also gained market share as others exited the market. Stress is not an exception; it is an inevitable part of business cycles. FDOs survive and often emerge stronger because they are designed to do so. Flashy companies, built on appearances, crumble when the music stops.

The FDO Identity Test

Many organizations assume they are financially disciplined simply because their books are clean or their finance team appears competent. But appearances can mislead. The real question is whether discipline permeates leadership and culture.

A quick way to test this is through a simple question I call the **FDO Identity Test**.

Five Questions Every Leader Must Ask

1. Do financial discussions involve leadership beyond the CFO?
2. Are risks openly debated at the board level?
3. Are capital allocation decisions linked to long-term strategy?
4. Is cash flow reviewed as rigorously as revenue?
5. Does the organization celebrate prudence as well as growth?

If you can confidently answer "Yes" to four or five of these questions, your organization is on the path toward becoming an FDO. If your answers are mostly "No" or fewer than three are "Yes," your company is not financially disciplined; it is financially exposed.

1. **Doing FD**: Reviewing budgets, controlling expenses, and ensuring clean audits. Episodic and reactive.
2. **Being FD**: Embedding discipline into every decision, every level, every day. Continuous and cultural.

The FDO Identity Test is not a compliance exercise—it is a mirror. It forces leadership to confront whether financial discipline is truly embedded, or merely performed. Many companies will find that they are still operating on luck, momentum, or appearances. Recognizing this gap is the first step to building resilience.

I am advising a mid-sized services firm that had grown quietly and steadily for over a decade. It never sought headlines or explosive valuations. Instead, it built cash reserves, controlled debt, and expanded only when its core business generated a surplus.

When a recession hit, many of its larger, flashier peers fell into crisis. They over-leveraged, committed to unaffordable projects, and relied too much on borrowed money.

This firm cut spending early, was completely transparent with its vendors, and prioritized keeping customers happy. It survived and increased market share as its competitors went out of business. The discipline that was perceived as somewhat "conservative" in excess proved to be its most significant competitive advantage in a crisis.

Another example comes from a founder friend who had internalized financial discipline as a personal value.

Long before his company faced any external crisis, he embedded rigorous cash management, clear capital allocation rules, and transparent reporting. His team sometimes found his approach frustrating—why delay an expansion that investors were ready to fund? Why not stretch payables when competitors were doing so?

His answer was consistent: "If we cannot afford it with discipline, we should not do it." Years later, when funding markets tightened, his company stood out as one of the few that required no emergency restructuring. While peers scrambled, he stayed the course. His foresight was not luck; it was discipline practiced long before it became fashionable.

Contrast this with a high-profile startup I observed in the same period. It raised successive rounds of capital and was celebrated in the media as the "next big thing." The leadership leaned heavily on valuations as proof of strength.

Behind the scenes, however, there was no financial discipline. Cash was wasted on lavish offices, overpaid hires, and aggressive subsidies for customer acquisition.

When capital markets cooled, the façade cracked. Within a year, the company that had seemed invincible became a cautionary tale. The failure was not due to a lack of opportunity, but to a lack of discipline. Valuations can create appearances; only discipline creates endurance.

The most striking example for me personally was watching an FDO operate in real time during a crisis. This company faced a sudden regulatory shock that disrupted its core operations.

Instead of denial or delay, leadership immediately convened cross-functional teams. They reviewed cash flow daily, cut non-essential expenses within weeks, and maintained open communication with employees, suppliers, and lenders. The most remarkable aspect was cultural: decisions were not driven solely by finance.

Every department owns its financial role. Sales teams renegotiated credit terms. Operations adjusted procurement cycles. HR created retention plans that balanced morale with cost control. What I saw was discipline embedded at every level—an organization functioning as a single, cohesive system.

The outcome was predictable: while peers lobbied for bailouts or entered insolvency, this firm stabilized quickly and regained momentum. It reminded me that the essence of an FDO is not technical; it is cultural. These stories underscore a single truth: appearances can be misleading, but discipline never is. Firms that practice discipline steadily, whether through governance, culture, or leadership design, are not merely surviving downturns; they are gaining strength from them.

Fragile firms may rise quickly, but they collapse just as quickly. FDOs, by contrast, may grow quietly, but they endure—and endurance is the ultimate measure of corporate success.

Culture, Structure, and Systems Reinforcement

Building a Financial Discipline Organization is not about a single pillar or initiative. It is about alignment. Culture, structure, and systems must reinforce one another. If even one is weak, the organization's resilience erodes.

Element	What It Represents	How It Works in an FDO	What Fails When It's Weak
Culture	The invisible rules that guide daily behavior	Employees internalize discipline; teams instinctively test decisions against long-term resilience rather than just short-term gain.	Systems are gamed, rules are bypassed, and discipline depends on enforcement rather than ownership.
Structure	Formal accountability and decision architecture	Ownership is separated from management; boards actively challenge capital decisions; checks and balances are embedded.	Governance devolves into rubber-stamping; authority concentrates; accountability blurs.
Systems	Technical enablers (ERP, reporting, audits)	Provide visibility, standardization, and consistency; reflect actual operational and financial reality.	Systems become polished facades; errors are amplified; weak behavior is automated.

Culture, structure, and systems do not exist in a vacuum. Together, they create resilience. That is what an FDO is all about - discipline that is reinforced on all sides, that leaves no place for indiscipline to occur.

A Financial Discipline Organization is not built on tactics. It is not about trimming expenses in a downturn, tightening reporting before an audit, or negotiating a better credit line. These may be helpful to practices, but they are episodic. An FDO is systemic.

It is an identity—a way of thinking and behaving that governs every decision, every day. Companies that persist across generations share one commonality: they were built with a purpose. Built means it's not luck or timing. Culture reinforces discipline, structure allows for accountability, and systems provide visibility. Together, organizations can build a resilience that is not dependent on a favorable landscape.

When considering this methodology, think of it as:

Name	Primary Focus	How Finance Operates	Organizational Outcome
Finance Department	Accuracy and compliance	Numbers are recorded, documented, and reconciled	Financial correctness, but limited strategic impact
Strategic Finance	Insight and decision support	Numbers are analyzed, interpreted, and used to inform decisions	Improved planning and performance, but discipline remains uneven
Financial Discipline Organization (FDO)	Resilience and sustainability	Numbers, culture, leadership, and incentives are fully aligned	Durable growth, predictability, and resilience under stress

This is the moment to reflect: Is your organization truly an FDO, or is it surviving on favorable conditions and market momentum? Are you building resilience intentionally, or waiting for discipline to be imposed by crisis? The difference is existential. One path leads to fragility disguised as success. The other creates endurance, trust, and long-term value.

5

THE FDO FRAMEWORK

Picture yourself with a rapidly growing company. In the past year and a half, your revenue has increased by twofold. Your sales pipeline is solid. You are gaining customers faster than ever. From the outside, this must be extraordinarily positive.

But behind the scenes, the company's expenses are threefold. Capital is getting more constrained because there's no natural cash flow coming from increased working capital to fund the additional expense. A variety of decisions that felt reversible are now permanent in their consequences. The company's risk exposure has quietly increased through its pricing, hiring, capital commitments, and vendor commitments, but its leadership remains confident because all dashboards appear normal. The company's finance department has years of experience and a high degree of competence. The company has implemented appropriate controls. Thus, on paper, the organization appears to be "doing well."

This contradicts many other leaders who say that high growth can easily amplify a business's weaknesses and not reward its strengths; growth not only tests the business's execution but also exposes flaws in its design.

What is commonly referred to as an "execution failure," about cost overruns, surprises relating to cash flow, or erosions in margins, is very seldom due to a lack of effort or a lack of competence; it's about the architecture of a business.

Most businesses do not fail due to a lack of viable intent; they do not fail despite a viable intent. Businesses do not fail because their leaders are uninformed; businesses do not fail despite a leader's competence. Businesses do not fail because they lack the right controls; they do not fail despite having the compliance boxes checked.

The core error is not obvious but has significant ramifications: financial disciplines are treated as a behavioral or moral issue rather than as a consequence of an overarching system. When financial discipline is defined at the individual level (whether through individual accountability, regulatory compliance, or financial talent), it becomes fragile; it relies on individuals behaving well, on external market conditions that are not volatile, and on pressure not being excessive. Once economic conditions are difficult (e.g., growth or stress), the concept no longer holds.

A critical distinction exists between Financial Discipline and Financial Control: Controls are mechanisms such as written policies, approval processes, and financial reporting. At the same time, Discipline is what you see as a constant relationship between the risk/reward/decision-making/behavior relationship over time. It is possible to have Controls without Discipline; however, you cannot have Discipline without having Design.

Discipline is not a catch phrase; it is a system; every system requires an architecture - an architecture that connects Corporate Strategy through to day-to-day decision making, connects individual financial performance to risk, and connects governance and controls and judgment into a unified whole.

Before we review the appropriate framework for financial discipline, it is important to understand why so many "good in-practice proposals" do not work in practice.

Why Most Attempts at Financial Discipline Fail

Many companies that struggle with financial discipline are aware of their financial discipline challenges. They've seen signs of trouble: tighter profit margins, longer cash cycles, and decision quality deteriorating under pressure. Typically, when companies have had time to react, executives/management will act on their gut and make a decisive move, but often end up with disappointing results due to misdiagnosis.

An example of this is the overconfidence of the leader(s) involved. The executive(s) believe they "know" the business well enough, based on their long experience or past successes, and therefore believe that discipline would slow momentum. The lack of resistance will often appear as decisiveness because you can make quick decisions, rely on your "gut instinct," and ignore "unnecessary" processes to reach execution faster. Over time, that overconfidence will erode the structure that would have identified risks before reaching a point of no return.

A second reason for failure is that many organizations believe financial discipline is a technical issue rather than an adaptive one. As a result, many organizations invest in new accounting and ERP systems and develop lengthy policy and procedure manuals, believing that these improvements will lead to greater discipline. However, the emergence of discipline within the system arises from rewards, behavior, and choice. If systems are introduced into the organization without first modifying how decisions are made and rewarded, they are treated as a layer of reporting rather than a layer of governance.

As we examine cultural fragmentation, the lack of financial responsibility stems from outsourcing financial functions. An operational leader who is focused on growth, delivery, or innovation will see any financial impact as someone else's issue. Even if organizations meet frequently, share dashboards, and distribute reports, decision-makers will still not be connected to the financial ramifications of their decisions. Therefore, discipline will show up episodically (in reviews) but not regularly (in day-to-day operations).

One of the main issues that many organizations encounter with compliance is called 'checkbox syndrome'. In this syndrome, judgment is replaced by compliance. Review processes have become a 'ritual'. External consultants deliver high-quality presentations, and their frameworks are adopted as principles. Initiatives are seen as complete; however, behaviors remain unchanged, decisions are not being made differently, risk is not being priced appropriately, and accountability is not improving.

All of these issues share one overarching aspect: they are all 'fragmented'. Leadership, culture, controls, and decision-making are being carried out in 'silos' (rather than as a complete 'system'). Thus, none of the 'financial levers' (i.e., quality of financial talent, strong controls, or the presence of a clearly defined governance structure) can compensate for the lack of true integration among them.

A lack of financial discipline does not originate from organizations having too little to try – rather, it's from trying to do it in parts. What is needed is an integrated, non-negotiable framework that works together.

Why Financial Discipline Needs a System

Financial discipline is often misunderstood as a function of finance, something enforced through budgets, policies, or periodic reviews.

In reality, discipline often fails due to a lack of rules within an organization, rather than to the rules themselves. In situations where financial transactions are controlled only by the vigilance of the finance group or by sporadic checks by leadership, discipline is unstable and lacks real strength.

Organizations tend to pursue multiple objectives simultaneously: growth, efficiency, and profitability. All of these areas are valid goals; however, issues can arise when growth initiatives are implemented without operational controls keeping pace with rapid expansion, or when efficiency programs do not take into account longer-range strategic goals.

Profit targets may be achieved temporarily while underlying financial risks accumulate unnoticed. When behaviors, processes, and economic outcomes are not aligned, financial discipline weakens—even in organizations with capable leaders and sophisticated financial reporting.

Sustainable discipline, therefore, requires more than policies or periodic interventions. To accomplish this, an integrated approach is required to create systematic processes for making decisions; executing work; and measuring results, and will also incorporate financial accountability—not just in the reporting of financial results, but through meaningful changes in leadership behavior, day-to-day operating processes, and economic decision-making.

The financial discipline framework was developed to create a unified structure of all the elements of financial discipline within an integrated organizational structure. Rather than creating financial discipline through a series of disconnected controls, the framework is intended to create an integrated system in which behavioral alignment, operating structure, and economic accountability are seamlessly aligned.

When these areas are aligned, financial discipline becomes an inherent part of the organization's decision-making process rather than an external constraint. Leaders make decisions based on their financial impact; processes support the execution of those decisions consistently; and financial results provide information for improvement.

To understand how this system functions in practice, it is useful to examine the **three dimensions of financial discipline** that shape the framework.

Financial Discipline Framework

Financial discipline becomes sustainable only when it is embedded across the organization rather than confined to the finance function. The Financial Discipline Framework organizes the disciplinary aspects of finance in an organization into three interrelated dimensions: People, Process, and Price.

These three dimensions work together as the structural logic that enables the mobilization of leadership intent through operational execution to achieve measurable financial results.

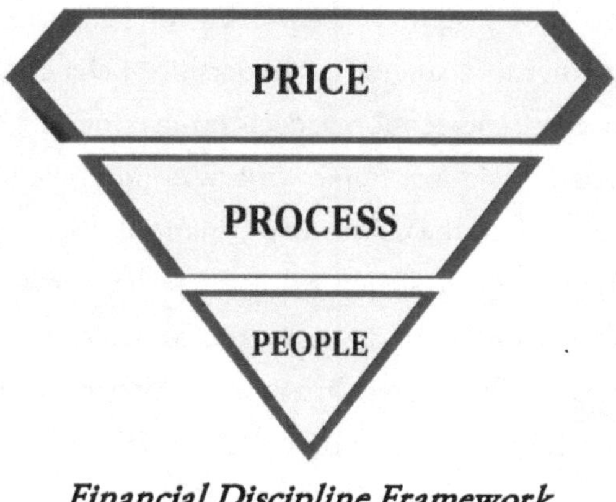

Financial Discipline Framework

People, the first dimension or starting point of financial discipline, are the underlying behavior related to it. Financial results are ultimately a reflection of the choices that individuals or leadership teams make. Each of the following factors shapes the choices made regarding finances (governance structures, leadership alignment, organizational culture, and personal accountability). When leaders demonstrate transparency, responsible resource stewardship, and long-term thinking, disciplined behavior becomes embedded in everyday decision-making. Without this behavioral foundation, even well-designed financial systems can be bypassed or ignored.

The second dimension, **Process**, represents the operational architecture through which discipline is executed. Decision-making processes determine the evaluation of decisions, the allocation of resources, and the monitoring of performance. Strategic Planning, Investment Decision Making, Budgeting, Risk Management, and Performance Measurement develop the structure that will direct the organization's activities. These systems provide consistency and transparency; therefore, financial objectives will not be integrated into operations after result reporting, but will already be included in operations throughout the course of doing business.

The third dimension, **Price**, indicates the economic dimension of business decisions. Financial discipline must ultimately be reflected in economic results. Pricing discipline, cost management, and capital efficiency ensure that the organization's strategic choices translate into sustainable financial performance. This dimension focuses on the quality of revenue, the structure of costs, and the effectiveness of capital deployment.

Importantly, these three dimensions do not operate independently. Financial discipline emerges from their interaction. The behavior of leaders affects how an organization performs, while how well an organization does business depends on the processes used to evaluate economic outcomes. When these three aspects (Leaders, Processes, Economic Outcomes) are aligned, they help create a unified system that facilitates disciplined growth and creates long-term value for the organization.

Many organizations have strong capabilities within only one of the three dimensions and often neglect to develop or improve upon the others. For example, organizations can develop strong operational processes but lack accountability to their employees for creating the desired culture, or have disciplined financial processes but lack disciplined leaders and a strong culture, or have disciplined leaders and a strong culture but poorly defined processes to evaluate economic outcomes. Sustained financial discipline occurs only when the three dimensions of People, Processes, and Prices are successfully integrated into a single system to achieve the desired results.

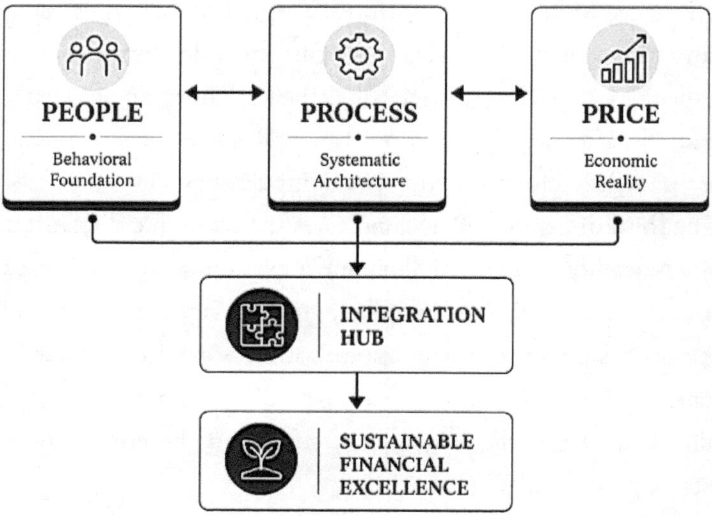

Integration Overview: Financial Discipline Framework " 3P MODEL."

The first of these dimensions begins with the human side of financial decision-making, the behavioral dimension of People.

People: The Behavioral Dimension

Financial discipline ultimately begins with people. Policies, financial systems, and reporting structures can guide behavior, but they cannot replace leadership judgment or organizational values. Every financial outcome — such as where to invest, how to spend, what price to charge, or how much risk to take — is affected by the choices made by people operating within a cultural and governing environment. Therefore, within the Financial Discipline Framework, the People dimension is viewed as the behavioral component on which disciplined decision-making is based throughout the organization.

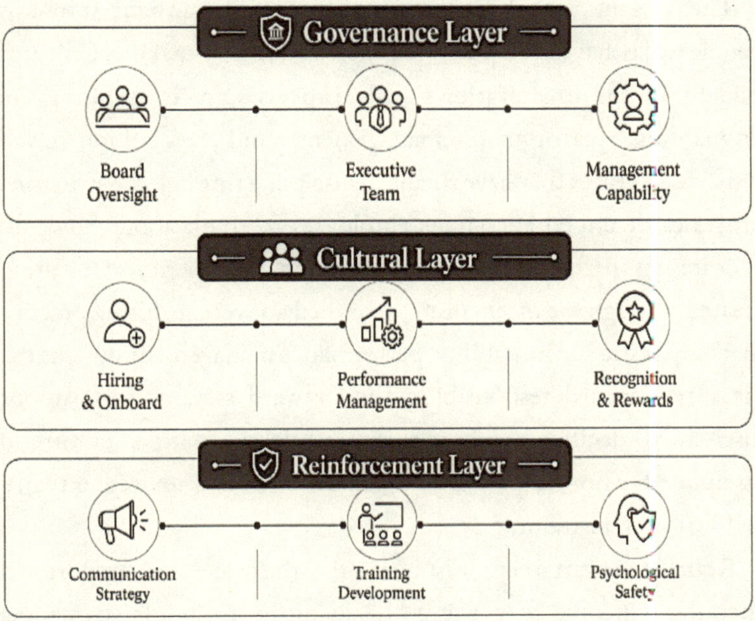

People Architecture: Behavioral Foundation

Within this dimension, financial discipline is shaped through three reinforcing layers: governance, culture, and reinforcement. Together, these layers determine how consistently disciplined behavior is practiced and sustained.

The Governance Layer defines the leadership structure responsible for keeping financial discipline.

Governance provides accountability for financial performance and provides strategic stewardship. Typical components include board oversight, alignment of executive teams with the organization's financial realities, and management's ability to translate strategic priorities into disciplined operational decisions. When functioning effectively, the governance structure allows financial decisions to be assessed for both their short-term and long-term impacts.

The Organizational **Culture Layer** provides insight into how people will behave in response to financial decision-making. Culture is evident in the organization's daily processes, such as hiring and onboarding, performance management, and recognition/reward systems. Cultures that have financial discipline through the structured processes described encourage employees to think about how they allocate resources and achieve operational efficiency. Culture is created through the mechanisms described above, e.g., hiring practices that emphasize accountability, performance management systems that measure financial responsibility, and reward systems that support disciplined decision-making; together, these create a culture of discipline as a normal part of an organization's behavior, rather than as an imposed constraint.

Reinforcement mechanisms are the third level of support that encourages people to continue behaving in a disciplined manner. Good governance and good culture can erode over time without reinforcement through ongoing communication strategies, leadership messaging, and transparent communication of financial performance. Financial training is also provided, enhancing financial literacy and decision-making capabilities across the organization. Equally important is psychological safety—an environment in which individuals can raise financial concerns, question assumptions, and report potential issues without fear of negative consequences

Key Behaviors:

- Conservative decision-making
- Transparency
- Long-term thinking
- Accountability
- Resource stewardship
- Continuous learning

When these three layers operate together, they encourage several critical behavioral outcomes: transparency in financial information, accountability in resource allocation, long-term thinking in strategic decisions, and responsible stewardship of capital. These behaviors create the human foundation upon which financial discipline depends. However, behavioral alignment alone is not sufficient. For discipline to be sustained, it must also be embedded in the operational systems and routines that guide how organizations work every day.

Process: The Operational Dimension

While leadership behavior establishes the foundation of financial discipline, discipline becomes meaningful only when it is translated into **structured organizational processes**. The operational component of the framework on financial discipline is one of three and centers on operational decisions, operational resources, and how operations are measured. Simply put, even the best and most responsible organizational leaders can struggle to maintain consistent financial discipline within a larger, more diverse organization if financial discipline is not established through defined processes.

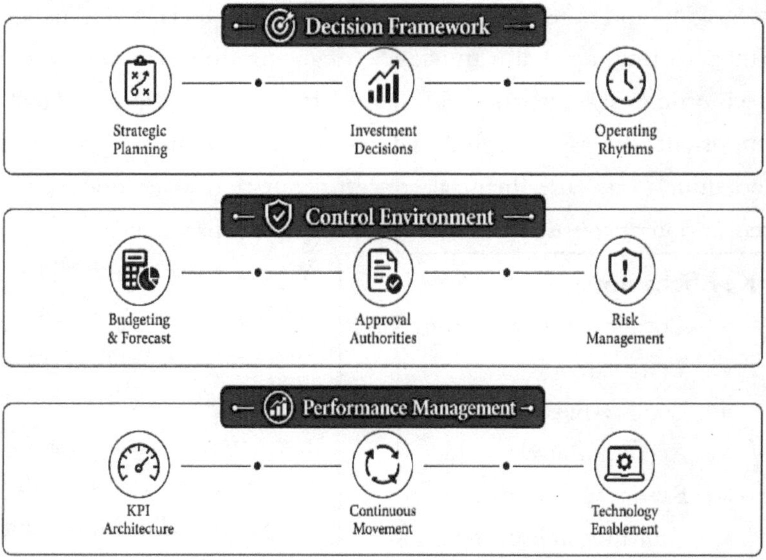

Process Architecture: Systematic Architecture

This operational dimension organizes financial discipline through three core layers: the decision framework, the control environment, and performance management. Together, these layers ensure that disciplined thinking is embedded in the organization's everyday mechanics.

The **decision framework** defines how organizations evaluate strategic and operational choices. Financial discipline requires that significant commitments—such as investments, expansions, or major operational initiatives—be evaluated through a structured process rather than on an informal basis. Strategic planning processes provide direction by linking long-term goals to resource allocation. Capital investment decision frameworks will ensure capital is allocated to projects that create ongoing value. The established operating rhythms, including regular planning and review cycles, support disciplined decision-making by providing routine and predictable opportunities to evaluate results and take corrective action as needed.

They are also a way to ensure that financial considerations remain the primary basis for all strategic and operational decisions.

The second layer, the **control environment**, establishes the boundaries that protect financial stability. Controls create the guardrails within which organizational decisions are made. Financial performance and resource allocation can be assessed within an organization using budget and forecasting systems. Approval authority for a financial resource commitment made at various levels of the organization. The matrix below illustrates how financial decision authority can be structured across leadership levels to ensure that commitments scale with organizational oversight.

Decision Authority Matrix

Amount Range	Individual	Supervisor	Manager	Director	VP	CEO	Board
< $1K	■						
$1K – $5K		■					
$5K – $25K			■				
$25K – $100K				■			
$100K – $500K					■		
$500K – $2M						■	
> $2M							■

Legend: ■ = Approval Authority

Organizations can use risk management frameworks to identify potential financial risks and address them before they negatively impact stability. These controls also help ensure transparency, continuous monitoring of commitments made, and alignment between financial commitments and organizational priorities, thereby reducing the likelihood of uncontrolled expenditures or unmanaged risk.

The third layercomprises **performance management** systems that enable organizations to evaluate and monitor their results while supporting continuous improvement of their processes. Discipline requires that an organization not only make sound decisions but also assess whether the decisions have achieved their intended objectives.

The KPI architecture takes an organization's strategic objectives and converts them into measurable operational metrics. Continuous improvement methodologies also provide teams with opportunities to identify inefficiencies and strive for improvement over time.

Increasingly, performance monitoring technologies have provided organizations with real-time visibility into their financial and operational results, allowing management to detect problems sooner and respond more effectively.

Many operational practices will enhance financial discipline within your organization. Zero-based budgeting, rolling forecasts, automated controls, and real-time performance monitoring are just some examples of practices that can help an organization achieve accurate visibility into its financial performance while fostering disciplined decision-making.

Key Processes:

- Zero-based budgeting
- Stage-gate funding
- Rolling forecasts
- Automated controls
- Real-time monitoring
- Continuous optimization

When these operational systems function effectively, financial discipline becomes embedded in daily execution rather than enforced after the fact. Strategy is translated into consistent actions, and financial objectives remain visible throughout the decision-making process.

However, operational processes alone are not sufficient. For financial discipline to be meaningful, these processes must ultimately be grounded in **economic reality**—the financial outcomes that determine whether an organization creates sustainable value.

Price: The Economic Dimension

Financial discipline ultimately reveals itself in economic outcomes. While leadership behavior and operational processes shape how decisions are made, the real test of discipline lies in the financial results those decisions produce. The **Price dimension** of the Financial Discipline Framework focuses on the economic realities that determine whether an organization's strategy and operations translate into sustainable financial performance.

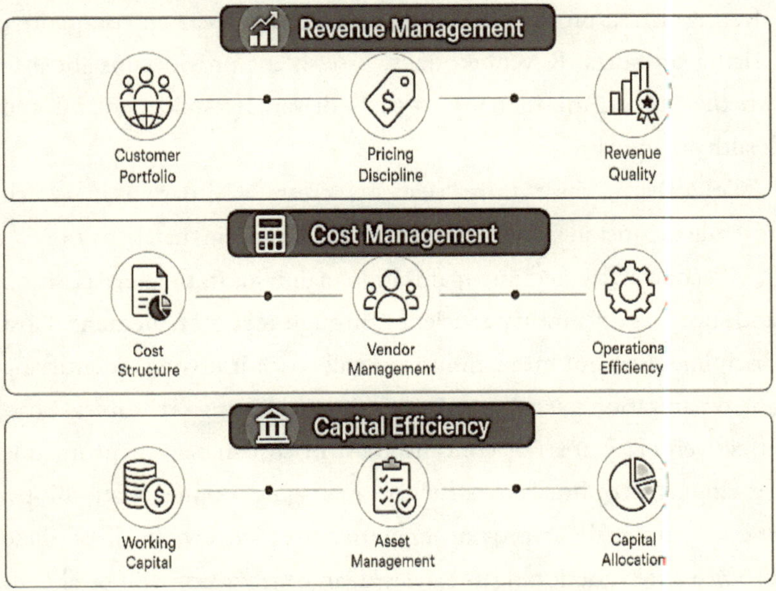

Price Architecture: Economic Reality

This dimension examines how organizations generate revenue, manage costs, and deploy capital. Together, these areas determine the quality of financial performance and the organization's ability to create long-term value.

Revenue management is the first area and is centered on generating income in a quality, sustainable way – something that requires financial discipline, which is about more than just increasing sales volume. Organizations need to ensure that revenue growth is consistent with sound strategic decisions and that it supports profitability. The major aspects of revenue management include customer portfolio management, pricing discipline, and revenue quality assessment. Customer portfolio management helps businesses deliver services and products to customers and segments that offer a long-term value proposition.

Pricing discipline helps businesses price product and service offerings based on their economic value rather than on competitive pricing pressures. Revenue quality assessment provides insight into whether an organization's growth is driven by solid demand and healthy margins.

Collectively, these three elements create a situation in which revenue expansion strengthens an organization's financial position.

A second area where an organization maintains its financial position and supports operational efficiency through **cost management**. Cost discipline does not mean eliminating all costs; it involves identifying an organization's cost structure and allocating resources cost-effectively. Key areas of concentration in cost management include developing an optimal cost structure, managing supplier relationships, and continuously improving operational efficiency. If all of these processes are functioning as expected, an organization will be able to keep costs under control while investing in the tools and resources necessary to support an organization's long-term growth.

Capital efficiency is another area of focus for an organization; it includes the efficient use of financial resources (e.g., assets) to generate revenue or profit. Strong capital efficiency management can help an organization avoid financial distress even when it is generating revenue or making a profit. An organization's financial management focus will need to include how well it manages (i.e., utilizes) working capital, fixed asset utilization, and whether it allocates its available capital resources effectively. Effective management of accounts receivable (AR), inventory, and accounts payable (AP) improves liquidity and increases cash flow. Successful management of an organization's assets enables it to receive a return on its investments. The strategic allocation of capital resources enables organizations to direct their financial resources toward the most significant value-adding activities over time.

To evaluate performance across these areas, the framework highlights several key metrics. Indicators such as customer profitability, the cash conversion cycle, return on assets, and free cash flow provide insight into whether financial discipline is producing sustainable economic results.

Key Metrics:

- Customer profitability
- Cash conversion cycle
- Price realization
- Return on assets
- Cost per unit
- Free cash flow

By focusing on these economic outcomes, the Price dimension ensures that disciplined behavior and structured processes translate into measurable financial performance and long-term value creation. However, the full strength of the framework emerges only when ***People, Process, and Price operate together as an integrated system***.

Integration: Aligning the Three Dimensions

The true strength of the Financial Discipline Framework lies not in the individual dimensions of People, Process, or Price, but in how they operate together as a coordinated system. Financial discipline becomes sustainable only when leadership behavior, operational execution, and economic outcomes reinforce one another. Without integration, organizations risk developing strong capabilities in one area while weaknesses in another undermine overall performance.

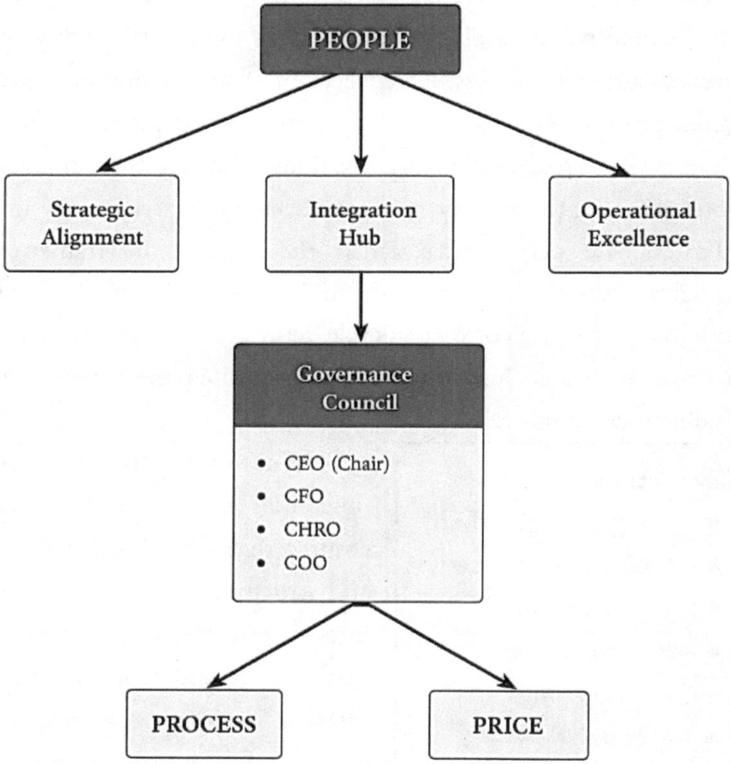

Integration Architecture: Making Dimensions Work Together

Mechanisms for integration will ensure that the three dimensions of your organization remain aligned throughout time. At the core of this integration is the structure of governance, which brings together all the leaders of your organization accountable for its activities (i.e., strategy, operations, talent, and financial oversight). Typically, this framework includes a governance council composed of a Chief Executive Officer (CEO), a Chief Financial Officer (CFO), a Chief Human Resources Officer (CHRO), and a Chief Operating Officer (COO).

Each role has a unique viewpoint representing a critical dimension of an organization (i.e., strategic direction, financial stewardship, people and culture, operational execution).

This type of leadership creates a forum that allows leaders to evaluate major decisions from multiple perspectives simultaneously.

Major initiative decisions are assessed for growth potential, operational feasibility, and financial sustainability. The evaluation of operational improvement initiatives is conducted from both an efficiency standpoint and a broader strategic perspective. Talent and cultural initiatives will be aligned with the behaviors needed to support disciplined financial management appropriately.

The interworking of the three dimensions will provide companies with a variety of cumulative benefits. Because employees see how their contributions support the organization's broader objectives, employee engagement has grown. When processes have better direction and accountability, employees will perform their tasks more effectively. Cost monitoring will be more effective when all decisions are evaluated against set financial limitations. Improved economic performance, driven by better discipline and systems, will result in greater cash flow.

In summary, integration enables an organization to shift financial discipline from independent controls to an integrated operating system for continual, disciplined growth. Companies can continually align their leadership, processes, and economic decisions to support sustainable performance, rather than reacting to financial results after the fact.

However, aligning these elements will require more than just structural integration; it will require establishing stable operating rhythms throughout the organization that support disciplined behavior and keep the framework active in day-to-day management.

Operating Rhythms

Financial discipline becomes sustainable only when reinforced by consistent organizational routines. Even well-designed frameworks can lose effectiveness if they are not embedded in the regular cadence of management activity. The Financial Discipline Framework, therefore, emphasizes **operating rhythms**—structured cycles of review and decision-making that keep financial priorities visible and actionable across the organization.

Financial Discipline Rhythms			
Daily	**Weekly**	**Monthly**	**Quarterly**
Cash check	Department review	Full P&L review	Strategic review
KPI alert	Forecast update	Variance analysis	Board reporting
Team huddle	Cross-functional discussion	Culture pulse	Framework update

These rhythms organize management attention across different time horizons, ensuring that financial discipline is monitored and reinforced continuously rather than only during periodic reporting cycles.

Organizations focus on operational visibility at the daily level. Cash monitoring, KPI alerts, and team coordination help detect potential issues early on. Daily checks enable quick feedback loops, allowing teams to resolve problems as they arise before they become larger financial issues.

Weekly attention turns to operational coordination and short-term performance management. Departmental reviews provide a way to evaluate current progress against targets, while forecasting updates help maintain a forward focus on financial performance. Discussions across all functions of the organization keep them aligned with and responsive to changing conditions.

Monthly reviews provide a more in-depth, comprehensive review of financial performance. Full profit-and-loss (P&L) reviews, variance analysis, and evaluation of cultural and operational indicators enable leadership teams to assess whether the organization's strategies and operations are producing the intended outcomes. These monthly reviews provide a structured way to identify deviations and make the required adjustments.

Finally, quarterly reviews are focused on strategic alignment and governance oversight. Strategic reviews, reporting to the board, and adjusting the framework for how the organization responds to changes in market conditions help to ensure that the organization stays aligned with its long-term goals.

Together, these operating rhythms create a management cadence that keeps financial discipline active across all levels of the organization. Rather than responding to financial outcomes after the fact, leaders can monitor performance continuously and intervene early when necessary. In this way, discipline becomes a **routine feature of organizational management rather than an occasional corrective exercise**.

Over time, organizations develop greater capability in maintaining these rhythms. As a result, financial discipline typically evolves through several stages before becoming fully embedded in the organization.

The Financial Discipline Maturity Journey

Financial discipline does not emerge fully formed. Organizations typically develop it gradually as leadership practices, operational processes, and economic management capabilities evolve. The Financial Discipline Framework, therefore, recognizes that companies progress through a **maturity journey**, moving from inconsistent practices toward deeply embedded, self-reinforcing systems of disciplined management.

The framework outlines **five stages of maturity**, each representing a different level of capability in sustaining financial discipline.

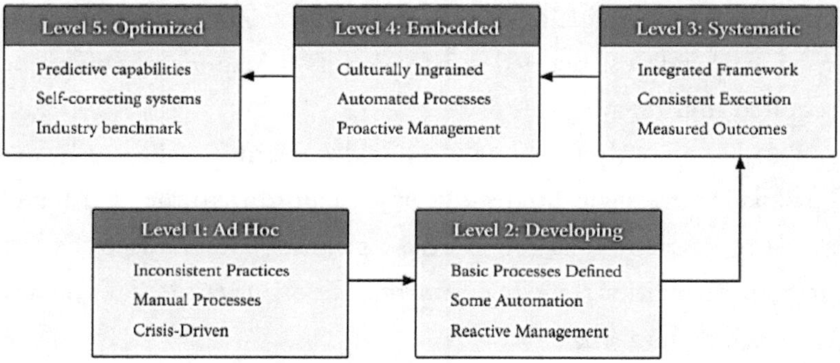

Financial Discipline Maturity Model

At the **Ad hoc** stage, financial practices are largely informal and inconsistent. Processes are often manual, and decision-making is frequently reactive. Financial visibility may be limited, and organizations tend to respond to issues only after they have already affected performance.

Organizations move into the Developing Stage as they become more formal in their approach to discipline. Basic documentation and processes emerge along with some automation. Yet discipline is still only partially applied across the organization, and management is largely reacting to subordinate behavior rather than proactively managing it.

The Systematic Stage represents a more structured approach to managing discipline. Organizations begin to develop integrated frameworks and apply consistent standards to the key business processes required to achieve financial discipline. The organization can now consistently track the results of the key business processes it manages, using data-based evidence to support its decisions.

Discipline is embedded in the organization's culture and operational systems at the Embedded Stage. The level of automation used at this stage varies, and the quality of discipline management continues to improve throughout the organization.

Anticipating issues before they occur becomes more feasible for management teams.

In the Optimized Stage, organizations develop advanced capabilities to proactively manage their discipline. Organizations can identify opportunities and risks prior to those opportunities and risks becoming reality through the use of predictive analytics, self-correcting systems, and by utilizing benchmark analysis against industry standards.

This progression illustrates an important insight: **financial discipline is not implemented through a single initiative or policy change**. Instead, it evolves through deliberate capability building, improved systems, and consistent leadership behavior. As organizations advance along this maturity path, the integration of People, Process, and Price becomes increasingly seamless, strengthening the organization's ability to sustain disciplined growth.

Financial discipline ultimately matters because of the value it creates. While the framework provides structure for leadership behavior, operational processes, and economic decision-making, its true significance lies in how these elements translate into measurable organizational outcomes.

Financial Discipline Value Creation Flow					
Inputs	**People (Capability)**	**Process (Execution)**	**Price (financial outcome)**	**Outputs**	**Outcomes**
Leadership Commitment	Leadership alignment	Structured decision-making	Revenue discipline	Better Decisions	Sustainable Growth
Clear Strategy	Cultural engagement	Operational coordination	Cost discipline	Higher Engagement	Competitive Advantage
Resources Allocated	Talent capability	Performance management	Capital efficiency	Faster Execution	Premium Valuation
Market Intelligence	Organizational learning	Process optimization	Pricing strategy	Lower Costs	Stakeholder Trust
Technology Platform	Data-driven mindset	Systems integration	Financial transparency	Better Margins	Long-term Survival
Cultural Readiness	Accountability culture	Continuous improvement	Investment discipline	Stronger Cash Flow	Sustainable Growth

These outcomes ultimately lead to sustainable growth, competitive advantage, and stronger stakeholder trust.

The Financial Discipline Framework begins with several critical organizational inputs. These include leadership commitment to responsible stewardship, clear strategic direction, disciplined resource allocation, and access to relevant market intelligence.

On their own, however, these inputs do not guarantee strong financial performance. Their effectiveness depends on how consistently they are translated into coordinated actions across the organization. This framework provides a systematic approach to achieve tangible results from the interrelated aspects of People, Process, and Price by aligning leadership and enhancing the organizational culture to provide better decision-making throughout the organization; establishing structured processes for operations results in quicker and more reliable executions of operations; and implementing economic discipline with respect to revenues, costs, and capital provides improved financial results by enhancing the management of cost and margin performance.

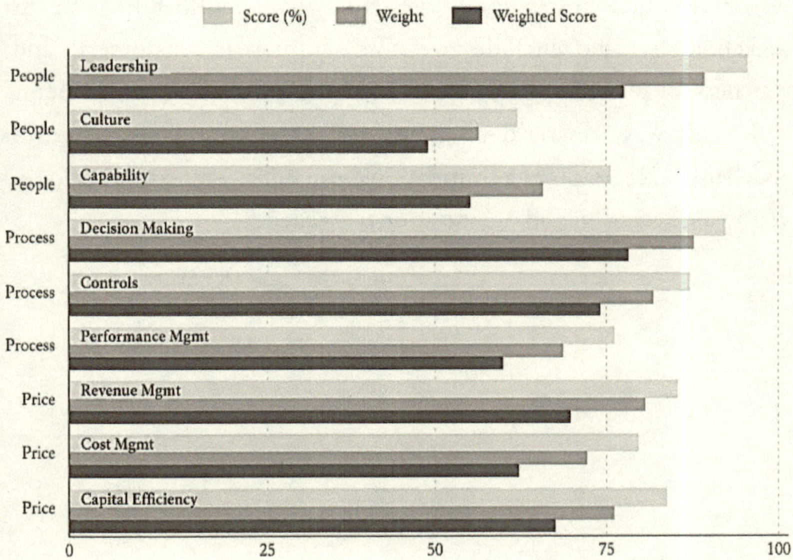

Using a scorecard, companies can define financial discipline in terms of measurable factors across the three dimensions listed above. This provides a comprehensive framework for an executive to leverage all three dimensions to create value for an organization.

In addition, as these organizations continue to improve their organizational discipline through scorecard measurement, they will also begin to benefit from broader strategic initiatives.

Financial Discipline Scorecard: Executive Dashboard

Continued disciplined decision-making will provide greater financial resilience; improved operational effectiveness will drive long-term profitability; effective deployment of capital will provide a competitive advantage; as these continue to improve on one another, they will create opportunities to grow the organization without compromising its financial stability. In summary, a disciplined organization will grow more sustainably, maintain its competitive advantage, and foster long-term trust and confidence with its stakeholders, who include investors, employees, customers, and partners, by providing evidence of responsible financial management.

In this way, financial discipline becomes more than a control mechanism. It becomes a foundational capability that supports long-term value creation and organizational excellence.

6

ASSESSING YOUR ORGANIZATION'S FINANCIAL DISCIPLINE QUOTIENT

Imagine a company that, by most visible measures, appears to be thriving. Revenue is growing steadily. Customer demand is strong. Investors are satisfied, and leadership meetings are filled with optimism about the future. The dashboards presented to the board show healthy margins, expanding market share, and confident forecasts. From the outside and even from within, the organization seems financially sound.

Yet beneath this appearance of strength, a different reality may be quietly developing.

Financial reports take weeks to finalize. Teams rely heavily on spreadsheets to reconcile numbers across departments. Important investment decisions are sometimes approved more based on urgency than of structured analysis. Certain individuals within the organization hold critical financial knowledge that few others fully understand. When questions arise about cash flow projections or profitability by customer segment, answers often require several days of investigation.

None of these issues appears alarming in isolation. Each can be explained away as a temporary inconvenience or the inevitable complexity of a growing organization. Because the company continues to perform well financially, leadership assumes the underlying systems are functioning adequately.

This assumption is common and dangerous.

Many organizations do not lack financial intelligence. They employ capable finance professionals, adopt sophisticated accounting systems, and produce detailed reports. What they often lack is diagnostic clarity: a structured way to evaluate whether their financial discipline is strong, fragile, or merely accidental.

Strong financial results can easily mask weak financial architecture. Growth can hide inefficiencies. Profits can obscure risks. And operational momentum can create the illusion that discipline exists where it has never been deliberately built.

In reality, financial discipline cannot be inferred from success alone. It must be observed in how decisions are made, how risks are managed, how resources are allocated, and how consistently the organization aligns behavior with financial reality.

This is where the Financial Discipline Quotient (FDQ) becomes essential.

The Financial Discipline Quotient is a diagnostic measure that evaluates the depth and maturity of financial discipline within an organization. Rather than focusing solely on outcomes such as revenue or profit, FDQ examines the systems, behaviors, and decision-making structures that produce them. It provides leaders with a clearer understanding of whether their financial strength is sustainable or simply fortunate.

Every organization believes it is financially disciplined until its systems are tested by pressure, uncertainty, or rapid growth.

The purpose of the FDQ is to ensure that such tests reveal resilience rather than fragility.

What is the Financial Discipline Quotient (FDQ)?

If financial discipline is the capability that sustains an organization through growth, competition, and uncertainty, then leaders need a way to understand how strong that capability truly is. The Financial Discipline Quotient (FDQ) provides that understanding.

The Financial Discipline Quotient can be thought of as an organization's *financial fitness score.* FDQ evaluates the internal strength of an organization's financial systems and behaviors. A company may look healthy based on revenue or profitability, but the FDQ asks a deeper question: How capable is the organization of consistently making sound financial decisions over time?

Traditional financial metrics measure outcomes. They tell leaders what has already happened: revenue earned, profit generated, costs incurred, or assets accumulated. These measures are important, but they are fundamentally backward-looking. They describe the results of past decisions rather than the quality of the systems that produced those decisions.

FDQ focuses instead on financial capability. It examines whether the organization possesses the structural and behavioral foundations necessary to sustain disciplined decision-making in the future.

In other words, while financial statements reveal performance, FDQ evaluates readiness and resilience.

This diagnostic perspective matters because strong outcomes can sometimes coexist with weak underlying discipline. Favorable market conditions, temporary demand surges, or aggressive growth strategies can produce impressive results even when internal financial practices are inconsistent. When conditions change, however, organizations lacking disciplined systems often struggle to adapt.

The FDQ therefore evaluates three underlying elements that shape financial performance:

- **The behavior of** how leaders and teams make financial decisions and allocate resources
- **Systems**, processes, and tools used to manage financial information
- **Decision architecture** is the governance structures that guide risk, investment, and accountability

Why Financial Discipline Must Be Measured

Most organizations believe they are financially disciplined. Leadership teams often assume that because the company is profitable, growing, or meeting its targets, the underlying financial systems must be functioning effectively. This belief is understandable, but it is also one of the most common sources of hidden organizational risk.

The danger lies in assuming discipline rather than measuring it.

Financial performance can remain strong for extended periods even when underlying processes are weak. Favorable market conditions, rapid demand growth, or strong product-market fit can mask inefficiencies and poor decision structures. As long as revenue continues to rise, the organization may never feel the urgency to examine whether its financial foundations are truly sound.

A powerful psychological force reinforces this illusion: overconfidence bias. Leaders who have successfully grown a business or navigated previous challenges often develop confidence in their instincts and judgment. That confidence can become a strength, but it can also create blind spots. When results are positive, it is easy to attribute success to strong discipline rather than to favorable circumstances.

This dynamic helps explain why leadership teams frequently overestimate their organization's financial resilience. Without structured measurement, leaders rely on signals that may seem reassuring but do not reflect the system's underlying health.

Part of the problem lies in traditional financial metrics. Most organizations rely heavily on lagging indicators, such as revenue growth, profit margins, or quarterly earnings. These indicators describe outcomes that have already occurred. By the time they reveal a problem, the decisions that created that problem have already been made. Financial discipline, however, is fundamentally about future reliability, not past performance.

To evaluate reliability, organizations must examine leading indicators, the processes, controls, and behaviors that shape how decisions are made before results appear in financial statements. Weak forecasting processes, inconsistent decision authority, unclear cost accountability, or fragmented reporting systems may not immediately affect profitability, but they signal fragility that can surface later under pressure.

This is where the Financial Discipline Quotient (FDQ) plays a crucial role.

Why Traditional Metrics Can Mislead Leaders		
Dimension	**Traditional Financial Metrics**	**Financial Discipline Quotient (FDQ)**
Focus	Past financial outcomes	Future decision reliability

Type of Indicators	Lagging indicators	Leading indicators
Typical Measures	Revenue growth, profit margins, and quarterly earnings	Forecast quality, decision governance, cost accountability, and reporting discipline
Insight Provided	What happened	Why it happened and how reliable the system is
Risk Visibility	Problems appear after the fact	Risks are visible before they become financial losses
Leadership Perception	Often reinforces overconfidence	Encourages objective assessment

Traditional metrics show what happened. The FDQ helps leaders understand how reliably the organization will perform in the future.

By measuring the systems, behaviors, and decision structures that influence financial outcomes, the FDQ reveals vulnerabilities long before they appear in financial results. It provides early warning signals, helping organizations identify weaknesses while there is still time to strengthen them.

In this sense, measuring financial discipline is not an exercise in criticism or compliance. It is a way of protecting the organization's future by ensuring that today's success is supported by systems strong enough to withstand tomorrow's uncertainty.

The Self-Assessment Paradox

Assessing financial discipline requires more than analytical tools. It requires a particular mindset from leadership, one that is often difficult to adopt. The challenge arises from a paradox: the leaders most capable of building disciplined organizations are often the same leaders who find it hardest to question their own systems. Successful executives develop strong confidence in their judgment.

Over time, that confidence becomes an essential part of leadership identity. When organizations grow under their direction, it is natural to assume that internal processes are functioning well. As a result, attempts to assess financial discipline can feel less like an operational review and more like a challenge to leadership competence. This is why many leaders resist honest self-assessment, even unintentionally.

Several psychological dynamics reinforce this resistance. Ego protection encourages leaders to interpret information in ways that confirm their existing beliefs. Success bias leads teams to attribute positive outcomes to internal strengths rather than external circumstances. And distance from operational reality means that senior executives often see polished reports rather than the daily workarounds that employees use to keep systems functioning.

These forces create a gap between perception and reality. From the leadership perspective, financial management may appear orderly and controlled. From a technical operational perspective, teams may rely on manual fixes, informal approvals, and undocumented processes to keep things running.

Closing this gap requires a fundamental shift in mindset.

Instead of viewing assessment as a means to prove competence, leaders must treat it as a means to identify weaknesses. The goal is not to confirm that the organization is disciplined; the goal is to understand where discipline is fragile so that it can be strengthened.

Several mental models can help leaders adopt this perspective.

One useful approach is to imagine viewing the organization through the eyes of a new executive or external investor. What financial practices might appear unclear or inconsistent to someone encountering them for the first time? Another approach is the "pre-mortem" exercise, asking what internal weaknesses could cause the organization to struggle during a future downturn or rapid expansion.

Leaders can also ask themselves a set of simple but powerful questions:

- Where do financial answers take longer than they should?
- Which processes depend heavily on specific individuals rather than systems?
- How quickly could we detect a significant financial problem if one were to emerge?
- Which financial assumptions have we accepted without recently verifying?

These questions are not meant to create doubt in leadership capability. Instead, they encourage a habit that distinguishes resilient organizations from fragile ones: the willingness to examine strengths and weaknesses with equal honesty.

Financial discipline begins not with systems or controls, but with awareness. When leaders are willing to examine their organizations without defensiveness, they create the conditions necessary for discipline to evolve from aspiration into reality.

The FDQ Self-Assessment Tool

Assessment only matters if it can be used. The FDQ Self-Assessment Tool is designed to reduce the gap between insight and action, moving the conversation from abstract agreement to concrete reflection. It is intentionally simple in form but demanding in its implications.

The tool consists of a checklist of 15 to 20 diagnostic statements, each describing a specific financial behavior rather than a policy or system. Respondents are asked to assess whether each statement is *consistently true*, *partially true*, or *generally untrue* for their organization. The emphasis is on consistency, not aspiration.

The diagnostic areas span the full discipline system. They include leadership involvement, whether senior leaders actively model disciplined trade-offs rather than intervening ad hoc. They examine cash visibility, whether liquidity is understood in real time or reconstructed after the fact. They test escalation clarity, whether people know when and how to raise financial risk without fear. They prob the risk discussion cadence, whether risk is surfaced proactively or only after outcomes are known. They assess cultural responses to bad news, whether transparency is rewarded or quietly penalized.

Once responses are complete, scores are aggregated to produce an overall FDQ range rather than a precise number. Scores below 40 indicate Chaos risk, where discipline depends heavily on individuals. Scores from 40 to 60 suggest Fragile control, where tools exist but behavior is inconsistent. Scores between 60 and 80 reflect structured but exposed organizations, systemic, yet vulnerable under stress. Scores above 80 signal Embedded discipline, where financial behavior is predictable and resilient.

The tone of the tool is critical. This is not an audit, nor a performance evaluation. It is a shared mirror. The value lies less in the score itself than in the conversations it provokes, where perceptions diverge, where assumptions surface, and where reality becomes discussable.

FD Quotient Self-Assessment Checklist

How to use this tool: Read each statement carefully and rate how true it is for your organization *in practice*, not in intent.

Score each statement as:

- 5 = Consistently true
- 3 = Sometimes true/inconsistent
- 1 = Rarely true or untrue

Avoid debating edge cases. Your first instinct is usually the most accurate.

Leadership & Governance	Score
1. Senior leaders actively engage in financial trade-off decisions rather than delegating them entirely to finance. 2. Decision rights around spending, risk, and escalation are clearly defined and respected. 3. Financial concerns can be escalated without fear of political or personal consequences. 4. Governance forums challenge assumptions rather than rubber-stamping proposals.	
Cash & Financial Visibility 5. Cash position and short-term liquidity are visible and understood without retrospective reconstruction. 6. Revenue growth is regularly evaluated alongside margin, cash impact, and delivery effort. 7. Forecasts are treated as decision tools, not as formal reporting. 8. Variances trigger inquiry and learning, not blame or justification.	
Operational Controls & Execution Discipline 9. Financial controls are embedded in operational workflows, not layered on afterward. 10. Exceptions to controls are rare, documented, and reviewed, not normalized. 11. Performance pressure does not routinely override agreed financial safeguards.	

12. Controls are designed to surface risk early, not merely explain outcomes later.	
Risk Intelligence & Decision Rhythm 13. Financial and operational risks are discussed proactively and regularly. 14. The organization distinguishes clearly between normal decision rules and crisis rules. 15. Risk is consciously priced and accepted, not retrospectively justified.	
Culture & Behavioral Alignment 16. Bad financial news travels faster than good news. 17. Incentives align with long-term value creation, not short-term metric optimization. 18. Financial discipline is viewed as a shared organizational responsibility not "finance's job."	
Total Score	

Interpreting Your Score

Below 40 (Chaos Risk): Discipline depends on individuals. Outcomes are unpredictable under stress.

40–60 (Fragile Control): Tools and policies exist, but behavior is inconsistent and easily overridden.

60–80 (Structured but Exposed): Systems are in place, yet discipline weakens during growth or pressure.

80+ (Embedded Discipline): Financial behavior is predictable, resilient, and reinforced by the system.

Why Organizations Feel "Fine" Until Crisis Hits

Many organizations operate for years, believing that their financial systems are stable and effective. Revenues are growing, customers are satisfied, and operations continue without major disruption. From the leadership perspective, there is little evidence that anything is fundamentally wrong.

Yet in many cases, this sense of stability is less a sign of strong discipline and more a reflection of favorable conditions. When markets are expanding and demand is strong, weaknesses within the organization can remain hidden for long periods.

One of the most common masking forces is growth itself. Rapid expansion often generates enough revenue to absorb inefficiencies that would otherwise be visible. Processes may be slow, approvals inconsistent, or cost structures poorly understood, but rising income can offset these problems. Because performance indicators remain positive, leadership assumes the underlying systems must be working.

Another source of hidden fragility is the presence of hero-dependent processes. In many organizations, certain individuals quietly compensate for weaknesses in systems and controls.

A senior accountant may reconcile inconsistencies manually each month. An experienced operations manager may detect pricing errors before they reach customers. A long-tenured employee may know how to extract critical information from outdated systems. These individuals become informal safeguards that keep the organization functioning. As long as they remain in place, structural weaknesses remain invisible.

Calm economic conditions can reinforce this illusion. When markets are stable and financing is available, the pressure on financial systems is relatively low. Processes that would struggle under volatility can appear adequate during periods of predictability.

Over time, operational workarounds, temporary fixes designed to solve short-term problems, have become normalized. Teams adapt to inefficiencies rather than addressing them, and these adaptations gradually become embedded in daily routines. The problem is that such systems have rarely been tested under real stress.

A sudden recession can expose weaknesses in cash forecasting and cost management. An external audit may uncover gaps in documentation or internal controls. The departure of a key executive can reveal how much critical knowledge was concentrated in a single individual. A technology failure may expose how dependent the organization has become on fragile manual processes.

When these shocks occur, the transition from apparent stability to visible crisis can be surprisingly rapid. What seemed like isolated operational inconveniences suddenly appear as symptoms of deeper structural problems.

Weak financial discipline seldom deteriorates visibly over time. More often, it stays concealed until external conditions shift. In reality, it doesn't weaken gradually but tends to collapse suddenly.

Organizations that seem financially stable in good times may find, during disruptions, that their financial resilience was overestimated.

The FDQ Diagnostic Model

If the Financial Discipline Quotient is intended to measure the strength of an organization's financial discipline, the next logical question is straightforward: what exactly should be measured?

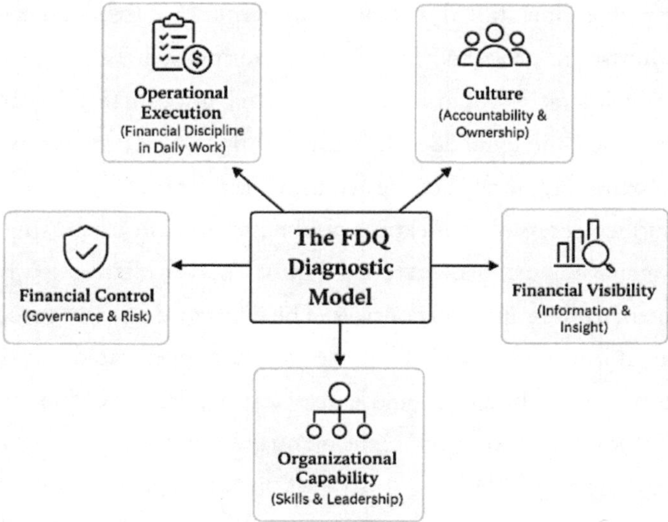

Financial discipline is not a single capability. It emerges from a combination of systems, behaviors, governance structures, and operational practices that together shape financial decision-making. To evaluate this complexity in a structured way, the FDQ assessment examines five foundational parts. Each part represents a critical dimension of financial discipline, and together they provide a comprehensive view of how effectively an organization manages its financial reality.

1. **Culture**

The first part evaluates the financial culture, the shared attitudes and accountability that shape how an organization handles its money. Strong discipline means everyone takes ownership. Leaders model stewardship, and teams routinely weigh costs and value in their daily decisions, making financial thinking a collective habit. Weak discipline happens when responsibility is siloed in the finance department. When budgets are seen as hurdles rather than commitments, even the best systems can't sustain disciplined behavior.

2. Financial Visibility

Financial discipline requires leaders to have clear, timely visibility into the organization's performance and risks. This part evaluates the effectiveness with which financial information is captured, analyzed, and communicated. Organizations with strong financial visibility can quickly understand key performance drivers such as profitability by product, customer segment, or geography. Financial data is accessible, timely, and structured to support decision-making. Weak visibility manifests as delayed reporting, incomplete information, or limited insight into operational performance. When leaders lack clear visibility, decisions are often made based on assumptions rather than reliable financial evidence.

3. Financial Control

The third part focuses on governance and accountability. Financial control evaluates how effectively the organization manages approvals, compliance, risk oversight, and internal controls. In disciplined organizations, financial responsibilities are clearly defined. Approval structures are transparent, and controls ensure that financial decisions follow established policies. Risks are identified early and monitored systematically. Weak control environments often rely on informal approvals, unclear accountability, or inconsistent enforcement of financial policies. Over time, this can lead to errors, compliance issues, or exposure to preventable financial risks.

4. Organizational Capability

Financial discipline also depends on the skills, experience, and collaboration of the people responsible for managing financial processes. This part evaluates whether the organization has the talent and capabilities required to support sound financial decision-making. Strong organizations invest in finance teams that combine technical expertise with strategic insight. Financial professionals collaborate closely with operational leaders, translating financial data into meaningful guidance for decision-making. Where capability is weak, finance teams may be under-resourced, overly transactional, or disconnected from operational realities. In such environments, financial insight remains confined to reports rather than influencing strategic choices.

5. **Operational Execution**

The final part examines how effectively financial discipline is embedded within day-to-day operations. Even the best financial systems and policies are ineffective if operational teams do not consistently apply them. Organizations with strong operational execution integrate financial awareness into routine activities such as pricing decisions, procurement, project management, and resource allocation. Financial considerations become a natural part of operational decision-making. Weak execution often appears when financial policies exist on paper but are inconsistently applied in practice. Operational teams may bypass processes to move quickly, creating gaps between financial strategy and operational behavior.

Together, these five parts provide a structured way to evaluate financial discipline across the organization. Rather than relying on impressions or isolated metrics, the FDO assessment examines the underlying architecture that shapes financial decision-making. By understanding strengths and weaknesses across these parts, leaders gain a clearer picture of where discipline is strong and where it needs strengthening to support sustainable performance.

Five Red Flags of Weak Financial Discipline

In many organizations, weaknesses in financial discipline do not appear immediately in formal reports or performance dashboards. Instead, they reveal themselves through subtle operational patterns, small signals that indicate deeper structural issues. Leaders who learn to recognize these signals can often identify problems long before they become serious financial risks.

The following five warning signs frequently indicate that an organization's financial discipline may be weaker than it appears.

1. **Constant Financial Surprises**

One of the clearest indicators of weak financial discipline is the regular appearance of unexpected financial outcomes. Budgets are missed without clear explanations. Forecasts require frequent revisions. Cash flow fluctuations catch leadership off guard. While occasional surprises are inevitable in any dynamic business environment, consistent unpredictability usually signals deeper problems. It may reflect weak forecasting processes, fragmented data systems, or a lack of alignment between operational decisions and financial planning. In disciplined organizations, financial outcomes may vary, but they rarely come as a complete surprise.

2. **Spreadsheet Dependency**

Spreadsheets are valuable tools, but when an organization relies heavily on them to manage core financial processes, they often become a sign of structural weakness. In many companies, critical financial information is assembled manually through complex spreadsheet models maintained by a few individuals. These models may combine data from multiple systems, require constant manual updates, and lack clear version control. Over time, such dependence creates operational risk. If a key file is lost, misunderstood, or incorrectly modified, the impact can spread quickly through financial reporting and decision-making. Strong financial infrastructure minimizes reliance on fragile manual processes by using integrated systems and standardized reporting frameworks.

3. Hero-Based Operations

Another common signal of weak discipline is the presence of "hero-based" financial management. In these environments, certain individuals become indispensable because they possess unique knowledge about critical financial processes. For example, a senior accountant may be the only person who understands how monthly reconciliations are completed, or a finance manager may hold the informal authority required to resolve pricing discrepancies. While these individuals often perform extraordinary work to keep the organization functioning, the system itself remains fragile. If these key people leave, take extended leave, or shift roles, the organization may suddenly struggle to maintain basic financial operations.

4. Month-End Chaos

The closing of financial books should be a structured and predictable process. When it becomes a period of intense last-minute activity, late nights, repeated adjustments, and urgent reconciliations, it usually signals deeper process weaknesses. Month-end chaos often arises from fragmented data flows, delayed reporting from operational teams, or unclear ownership of financial responsibilities. Teams spend significant time correcting errors or chasing missing information rather than analyzing performance.

Disciplined organizations design financial processes so that most work occurs continuously throughout the month, keeping closing periods controlled and efficient.

5. Leadership Disengagement from Financial Data

Finally, weak financial discipline often appears when leadership engagement with financial information becomes limited or superficial. In such organizations, financial reports may be produced regularly, but senior leaders rarely engage deeply with the data. Financial discussions focus primarily on headline numbers, revenue, or profit without exploring underlying drivers such as cost structures, working capital trends, or profitability by segment. When leadership attention remains at a surface level, opportunities for deeper financial insight are often missed. Over time, this distance can weaken the organization's ability to identify risks and make disciplined strategic decisions.

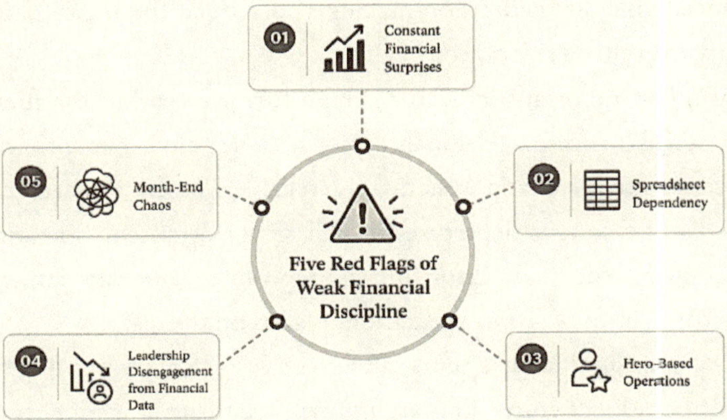

These signals may appear manageable. Together, however, they often reveal patterns that deserve careful attention. Recognizing these red flags early allows leaders to address weaknesses before they evolve into more serious financial vulnerabilities.

The Invisible Signals Leaders Often Miss

Beyond the visible red flags of weak financial discipline lie a set of quieter, often overlooked signals. These indicators rarely appear in financial statements or operational dashboards, yet they can reveal deeper structural issues within an organization's financial management systems. Because they emerge through behavior rather than numbers, leaders often underestimate their importance.

One such signal occurs when a founder or senior executive consistently bypasses the finance team during important financial decisions. While this may be driven by speed or confidence in personal judgment, it often reflects a deeper lack of integration between strategy and financial governance. Over time, such patterns weaken the role of financial analysis in decision-making and reduce the organization's ability to evaluate risk objectively.

Another important indicator is high turnover within the finance function. Finance professionals typically prefer environments where processes are clear and systems are reliable. When finance teams experience frequent departures, it can signal persistent operational frustration, such as disorganized reporting, unclear authority structures, or unrealistic expectations placed on the team.

Repeated audit adjustments can also serve as an early warning sign. While occasional corrections are normal, recurring adjustments may suggest weaknesses in internal controls, documentation, or financial processes. These patterns indicate that the organization's financial records may rely on post-facto corrections rather than on consistently reliable systems. Operational relationships can reveal additional signals. For example, vendor payment friction, frequent disputes, delayed payments, or inconsistent communication with suppliers often reflect underlying cash management problems or unclear approval processes. Over time, these tensions can damage external trust and limit operational flexibility.

Finally, the emergence of shadow reporting systems, independent spreadsheets, or unofficial dashboards maintained by different teams often indicates that official financial reports are not meeting operational needs. When departments create their own data sources, it suggests the organization lacks a unified, trusted view of financial performance.

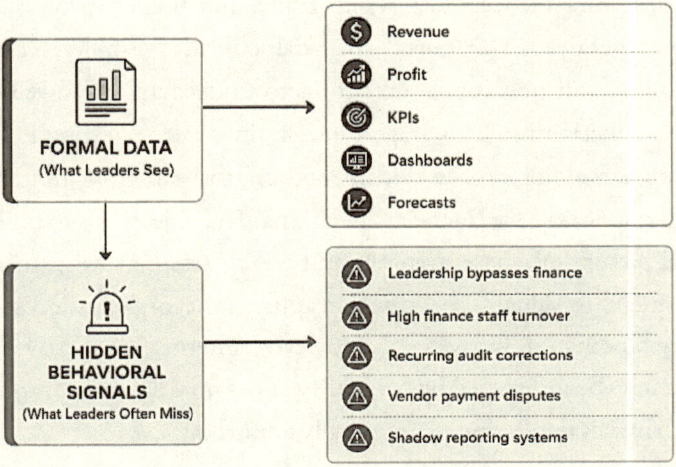

These signals are powerful because they reveal behavioral and structural weaknesses that traditional financial metrics may never capture. For leaders seeking to understand their organization's true level of financial discipline, paying attention to these subtle patterns can provide insights far earlier than any formal report.

How to Run an FDQ Assessment

Once leaders recognize the importance of measuring financial discipline, the next challenge is determining how to conduct the assessment to produce honest and useful insights.

Because financial discipline spans multiple systems, teams, and behaviors across the organization, an effective FDQ assessment should integrate different perspectives rather than rely on a single evaluation method.

In practice, the most reliable approach follows a **three-phase model**.

Phase 1: Internal Assessment — The process begins with an internal evaluation of the organization's financial systems, processes, and decision practices. Leadership teams and finance professionals review the five FDQ parts: financial culture, visibility, control, capability, and operational execution to understand how well each area is functioning. This stage typically involves reviewing existing reports, examining process documentation, and gathering input from teams responsible for financial operations. The objective is to build an initial picture of where strengths and weaknesses may exist. Internal assessment is valuable because it captures the organization's own understanding of its systems. However, internal perspectives can sometimes be influenced by familiarity or organizational assumptions, which makes the second phase equally important.

Phase 2: External Validation — External validation introduces an independent perspective. This may involve outside advisors, auditors, or experienced financial consultants who review the organization's financial practices objectively. External reviewers often identify structural issues that internal teams may overlook because they have become accustomed to existing processes. They can also benchmark the organization's practices against industry standards and leading financial management approaches. The purpose of this phase is not criticism but clarity, ensuring that the organization's self-assessment accurately reflects its true level of discipline.

Phase 3: Joint Improvement Roadmap — The final phase combines insights from both internal and external perspectives to develop a practical improvement plan. Leaders identify the most critical gaps in financial discipline and prioritize actions that will strengthen systems, processes, and decision-making structures. This joint roadmap ensures that improvement efforts remain realistic and aligned with organizational priorities. Rather than attempting to transform everything at once, the organization focuses on the changes that will have the greatest impact on resilience and performance.

A hybrid assessment approach works best because it balances internal knowledge with external objectivity. Internal teams understand operational realities, while external perspectives challenge assumptions and highlight blind spots. Together, they create a more accurate and actionable understanding of the organization's Financial Discipline Quotient.

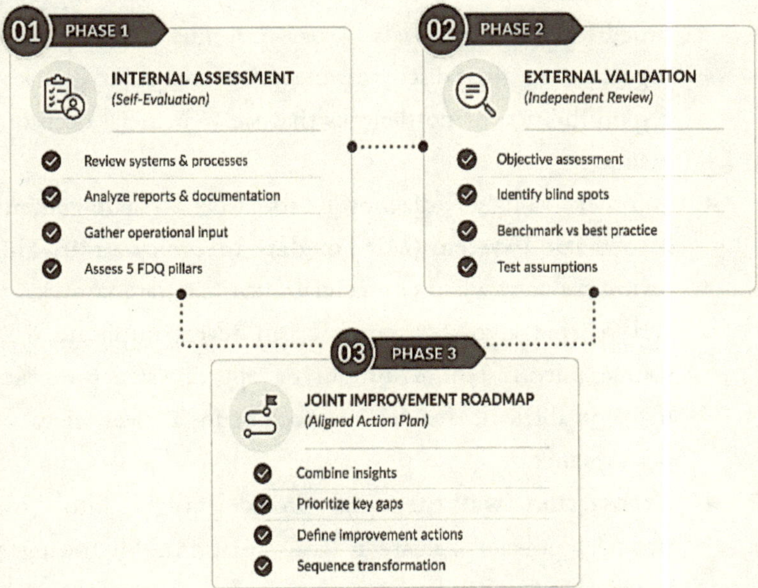

Tools for Diagnosing Financial Discipline

Conducting an FDQ assessment requires more than reviewing financial statements. Because financial discipline is embedded in systems, behaviors, and operational routines, leaders must use diagnostic tools that reveal how these elements function in practice.

Several practical methods can help uncover hidden weaknesses.

- **Anonymous leadership surveys** are often a useful starting point. When senior leaders and department heads are invited to share candid perspectives about financial processes, they frequently highlight issues that formal reports do not capture. Anonymous feedback encourages honesty and helps identify areas where financial systems may not be supporting operational needs.

- **Process mapping workshops** help teams visualize how financial information and decisions flow through the organization. By mapping processes such as budgeting, procurement approvals, or revenue recognition, organizations often discover unnecessary complexity, unclear responsibilities, or bottlenecks that slow financial decision-making.
- Another valuable diagnostic tool is a **management information system (MIS) or data integrity audit**. This review evaluates whether financial data is accurate, consistent, and reliable across systems. It can reveal duplicate data sources, inconsistent definitions, or reporting structures that make it difficult for leaders to obtain a clear view of performance.
- **Transaction walkthroughs** provide insight into how financial policies operate in real situations. By tracing a transaction from initiation to approval to reporting, leaders can observe where controls are strong and where workarounds or informal practices have developed.
- Finally, **cross-functional 360-degree reviews** bring together perspectives from finance, operations, sales, and other departments. These discussions often reveal how financial policies are interpreted and applied across the organization. Differences in understanding can highlight areas where financial discipline has not been fully integrated into daily operations.

Tools for Diagnosing Financial Discipline		
Tool	**What It Examines**	**What It Reveals**
Anonymous Leadership Surveys	Leadership perceptions of financial processes and systems	Hidden frustrations, misalignment, and gaps are not visible in reports
Process Mapping Workshops	Flow of financial information and decision pathways	Bottlenecks, unclear responsibilities, and process inefficiencies
MIS / Data Integrity Audits	Accuracy and consistency of financial data across systems	Duplicate sources, inconsistent definitions, unreliable reporting structures
Transaction Walkthroughs	Real-life execution of financial policies and controls	Control strengths, workarounds, and informal practices
Cross-Functional 360° Reviews	How financial policies are understood across departments	Misinterpretations, integration gaps, and operational disconnects

Used together, these tools help leaders move beyond assumptions and gain a realistic picture of how financial discipline functions throughout the organization.

What to Do After You Know Your FDQ

Assessing the Financial Discipline Quotient provides leaders with something many organizations rarely possess: a clear picture of their financial reality. But diagnosis alone does not create discipline. The true value of the FDQ emerges only when its insights are translated into focused organizational improvement.

One of the most important principles at this stage is **prioritization**. Financial discipline affects many parts of an organization, and attempting to improve everything at once often leads to fragmented efforts and limited progress. Instead, leaders should approach transformation in a structured sequence.

- The priority is **addressing survival risks**. These are vulnerabilities that could immediately threaten the organization's financial stability if external conditions change. Examples may include weak cash flow visibility, inadequate internal controls, or unreliable financial reporting. Stabilizing these areas ensures that the organization can operate with basic financial confidence.
- Once immediate risks are addressed, the next focus should be on **structural stability**. At this stage, organizations strengthen the systems and processes that support disciplined decision-making. This may involve improving financial infrastructure, clarifying approval structures, standardizing reporting processes, or strengthening financial governance.
- Only after these foundations are secure should leaders shift attention toward **optimization**. Optimization initiatives aim to enhance efficiency and strategic performance, for example, improving cost management, refining pricing strategies, or strengthening financial forecasting capabilities.

To facilitate these upgrades, organizations can follow the same approach outlined earlier in the **Financial Discipline Organization (FDO) framework** discussed in Chapter 5. This framework highlighted three interconnected areas: **People, Process, and Price**. The transformation starts with People, ensuring that leaders and teams have the necessary financial understanding, accountability, and decision-making discipline to support improved systems.

Then, focus shifts to Processes, where organizations establish dependable structures for reporting, approvals, planning, and performance tracking. Lastly, organizations concentrate on Price, ensuring financial decisions are aligned with value creation, cost considerations, and market conditions.

Transformation Focus Matrix			
Priority Level	**People**	**Process**	**Price**
Survival	Accountability	Basic controls	Cash discipline
Stability	Capability building	Governance & reporting	Cost structure
Optimization	Strategic leadership	Performance systems	Value & pricing strategy

By approaching improvement through these interconnected layers, leaders ensure that financial discipline evolves systematically rather than through isolated initiatives. The FDQ assessment provides the diagnosis; the FDO framework provides the architecture for transformation.

The Timeline for Building Financial Discipline

Strengthening financial discipline is not a short-term project. It is a **capability that develops gradually**, as systems mature and behaviors become embedded across the organization. Leaders who expect immediate transformation often become frustrated, while those who understand the natural progression of improvement are better positioned to sustain change.

In many organizations, the journey follows a recognizable timeline.

During the first **0–3 months**, the main focus is typically on stabilizing operations. Leaders work to address the most urgent risks identified during the FDQ assessment, enhance cash flow visibility, clarify financial responsibilities, and fix critical reporting issues. From **3 to 9 months**, organizations start laying the groundwork. Financial processes are standardized, systems are reinforced, and governance structures are clarified. Teams shift from using workarounds to adopting more structured financial practices.

Financial Discipline Capability Curve

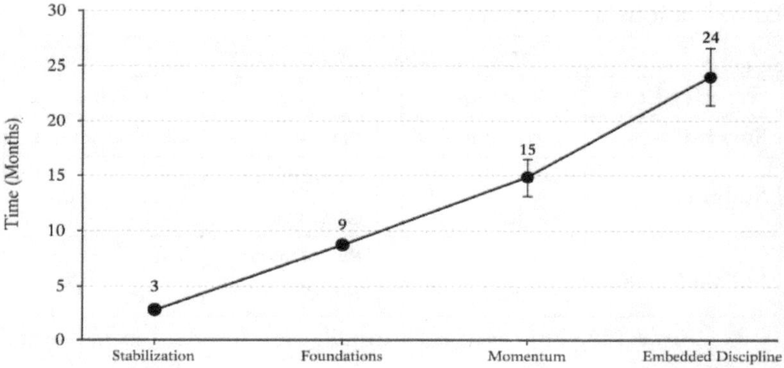

Between **9 and 15 months**, momentum tends to grow. Financial data becomes more accurate, decision-making improves, and operational teams begin incorporating financial awareness into their daily activities.

By **15 to 24 months**, financial discipline is often fully embedded. Systems run consistently, leaders rely confidently on financial insights, and financial accountability becomes integrated into the organizational culture. The key lesson is simple but important: financial discipline cannot be installed overnight. It develops through sustained attention to systems, processes, and leadership behavior. Organizations that treat discipline as a long-term capability rather than a quick fix are far more likely to build resilience that endures through growth, uncertainty, and change.

Organizations often begin transformation efforts with enthusiasm and urgency. Leaders invest in new systems, introduce policies, hire specialists, and launch initiatives designed to strengthen financial management. These actions are well-intentioned, yet many such efforts struggle to deliver lasting results.

The reason is simple: ***transformation frequently begins before diagnosis****.*

Without a clear understanding of their current level of financial discipline, organizations risk solving the wrong problems. They may invest heavily in sophisticated systems while underlying processes remain unclear. They may introduce new controls without addressing cultural behaviors that bypass them. In some cases, they attempt to replicate practices from highly disciplined organizations without recognizing the foundational structures that underpin those practices' effectiveness.

Financial discipline cannot be installed blindly. It must be built on a clear understanding of how the organization currently operates, its strengths and weaknesses, and the gaps between intention and reality.

The Financial Discipline Quotient (FDQ) provides this essential baseline. By examining the systems, behaviors, and decision structures that shape financial outcomes, the FDQ allows leaders to move beyond assumptions and develop a realistic picture of their organization's financial maturity.

Awareness, therefore, becomes the starting point for meaningful change. Once an organization understands its true level of financial discipline, the next challenge is not simply improving processes but embedding discipline deeply into how the organization operates. Leadership behavior, operational routines, and economic decision-making must begin to reflect the principles of disciplined financial management. In the chapters that follow, we turn our attention to this next stage of the journey: how organizations move from diagnosis to embedding financial discipline into the fabric of everyday decisions and actions.

7

BUILDING AN FDO CULTURE

Examining two companies at similar stages of development clarifies differences in financial performance when using a comparison framework based on the system complexity of both entities.

One company's systems tend to be complex and well-defined. The finance team has appropriate resources, policies are properly defined, and processes have appropriate accountability, oversight, and timeliness of reporting. Internal controls manage budgets, purchases, and capital expenditures. Controlling finances appears well-managed, as indicated by the documentation alone.

However, actual behavior indicates the contrary. Projects are expedited to spend down available budgets within a tight time frame leading up to the end of the quarter. Managers go through the process of approving policy exceptions rather than asking themselves whether the spending is warranted. Urgency is a great motivator in today's commercial arena, rather than adhering to a prudent economic plan. The Finance Group is responsible for managing financials, but this responsibility is considered the Finance Group's alone.

The second firm appears simplistic when compared to its counterpart.

The company's systems are simplistic, and the processes are less demanding. Many of the company's systems are not as sophisticated as those of its competitor; however, financial behavior is present on an everyday basis with respect to fiscal responsibilities.

Decision-makers routinely evaluate the cost of a decision against the overall value—company assets, whether tangible or intangible, are treated as assets available for use. Spend decisions go through a discussion and approval/denial process without conflict or unnecessary delays. Trade-off decisions are made and documented. The Finance Group does not just discuss the consequences of spending decisions. As the financial winds continue to shift, the two companies will remain in stark contrast: one with a well-developed system of controls, and the other with instinctive judgment governing behavior. One will maintain disciplined behavior during trying times, while behavior will continue to be determined by culture.

Financial Discipline Organizations succeed not because rules are stricter, but because discipline is internalized. When stewardship becomes instinctive, discipline no longer depends on supervision. It becomes the organization's default setting.

What an FDO Culture Really Means

Financial discipline becomes durable only when it is rooted in culture rather than enforced solely through oversight. In Financial Discipline Organizations (FDOs), culture functions as the invisible operating system that shapes how people think, decide, and act when financial trade-offs arise. It is not expressed through slogans or policy manuals, but through shared norms that guide everyday behavior. Culture determines whether financial responsibility is treated as a procedural requirement or as a professional obligation embedded in the organization's identity.

Core Components of an FDO Culture		
Component	**What It Ensures**	**Cultural Signal**
Structured Financial Governance	Clear principles, oversight, and accountability	Discipline is integral to leadership and performance
Data-Driven Decision Logic	Evidence-based evaluation of trade-offs and risks	Financial judgment is informed, not intuitive
Distributed Accountability	Ownership of financial consequences across roles	Stewardship is everyone's responsibility

Visible Behavioral Signals

Culture is observable in leaders' behaviors and is strongly influenced by them. For example, when senior leaders demonstrate personal fiscal restraint, they demonstrate that stewardship is expected from all levels of the organization. When leaders exhibit transparency in financial communication, it builds trust and provides a shared understanding of responsibility. Publicly acknowledging the efficient, prudent use of resources through financial transactions sends a signal that discipline is appreciated, not simply accepted. In addition to sending these signals through behaviors, the organization reinforces these signals through team behaviors as well.

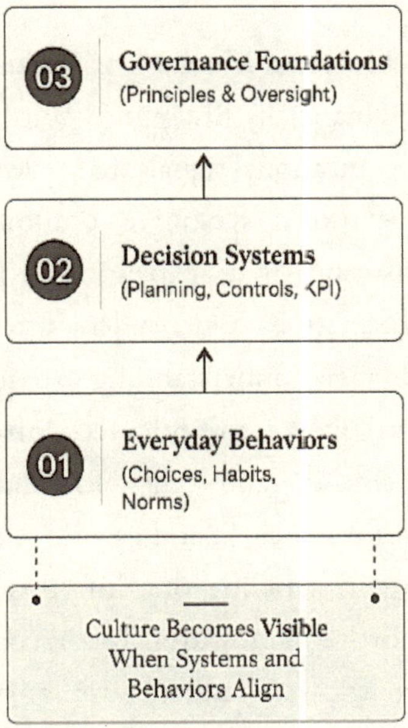

Cost awareness becomes part of the operational planning process, rather than a secondary thought or an added layer to the operational plan.

Budgets are planned based not only on their financial allocation, but also on the expected outcome.

Norms for sharing resources are established, thereby reducing unnecessary resource consumption and promoting collaborative effectiveness.

By reinforcing the organization's principles through visible behaviors, these principles can be translated from abstract concepts into reality, rendering financial discipline normative within the organization rather than merely formal.

Cultural Markers of Financial Discipline

Financially disciplined cultures become visible through consistent organizational signals that reflect how stewardship is practiced in daily operations. Resource optimization is valued alongside growth, ensuring that expansion efforts are pursued with efficiency expectations and prudent use of capital rather than volume alone. Financial understanding extends beyond the finance function, with employees across roles recognizing the economic implications of their decisions and the fundamentals that shape organizational performance. Spending priorities remain closely aligned with strategic intent, avoiding the drift that often arises from legacy patterns or short-term pressures. Teams continuously refine processes to improve workflows, eliminate waste, and strengthen cost-effectiveness, treating efficiency as an ongoing responsibility rather than a periodic initiative. Most importantly, financial outcomes are regarded as a shared responsibility, reinforcing the view that stewardship is collective and not confined to a single department or leadership layer.

Marker	What It Looks Like in Practice
Resource Optimization with Growth	Expansion decisions balance scale with efficiency and prudent capital deployment.
Organization-Wide Financial Literacy	Non-finance teams understand unit economics, cost drivers, and value creation logic.
Expense-to-Strategy Alignment	Spending patterns reinforce strategic priorities rather than legacy habits.
Continuous Process Refinement	Teams routinely remove waste, streamline workflows, and improve cost-effectiveness.
Shared Ownership of Outcomes	Financial performance is treated as a collective responsibility across functions.

Culture or Compliance

Financial discipline and compliance are frequently treated as the same, even though they represent distinct concepts. Because of this widespread confusion, organizations frequently spend significant time and money developing policies, approval processes, audit protocols, and reporting tools to create a tight control environment that will lead to the automatic development of disciplined behavior. While these structures and processes serve as essential precursors to disciplined behavior, they do not, in and of themselves, constitute financial discipline. Compliance is enforced by regulations that govern an organization's actions at designated checkpoints, whereas culture governs individual choices continuously. The distinction between compliance and financial discipline becomes obvious not during definitive reviews, but in the day-to-day decision-making activities that occur beyond the purview of management supervision.

As an example, when individuals internalize (i.e., embed) their financial responsibility, they can exercise their own judgment without waiting for direction; they can assess the trade-offs associated with their decisions without needing someone else to prompt them to do so; and they will use organizational resources as if they were entrusted to them for safekeeping. On the contrary, when financial responsibility is enforced, individuals' behavior is primarily dictated by supervisory approval, procedural barriers, and monitoring. Governance, then, will reinforce how someone behaves when discipline is embedded; however, when discipline is enforced, governance is trying to make up for a lack of it.

Behavioral Contrast: Embedded & Enforced Discipline

Real Culture Versus Policy-Only Organizations		
Dimension	**Real Discipline Culture**	**Policy-Only Environment**
Decision Making	Self-regulated	Approval-dependent
Spending Behavior	Value-seeking	Budget-exhausting
Accountability	Shared	Delegated to Finance
Leadership Signals	Modeled	Announced

In culturally disciplined organizations, people regulate themselves because expectations are clear and stewardship is normalized. Spending decisions prioritize value creation over allocation consumption. Financial outcomes are viewed as collective responsibilities rather than functional metrics. Leaders reinforce standards through visible personal conduct, not messaging alone. In policy-only environments, however, employees rely on procedural approval rather than internal judgment.

Budgets become spending targets, accountability narrows to finance teams, and leadership signals are delivered through communications rather than example.

The Litmus Tests

The presence of real discipline can be assessed through a few observable tests. Behavior when unobserved is often the clearest indicator; culture governs what people do when controls are distant. Conduct during periods of surplus reveals whether abundance weakens restraint, while conduct during constraint shows whether pressure erodes principles. Responses to financial stress, such as sudden revenue shocks or cost pressures, demonstrate whether discipline is situational or structural. Even onboarding experiences provide signals, as early norms teach newcomers what the organization truly values.

Financial discipline becomes visible in moments where policy is silent, and judgment takes over. Leaders can assess cultural strength by asking a few practical questions:

- When decisions are made without supervision, do teams still apply financial rigor?
- During periods of surplus, does spending discipline remain intact?
- Under constraint, are principles preserved or relaxed?
- When financial stress emerges, does the organization respond with structured action or reactive measures?
- What do new employees learn about resource stewardship in their first weeks?

The answers often reveal whether discipline is embedded in culture or dependent on controls.

Why Culture Outperforms Controls

Culture outperforms controls because it operates at the level of daily micro-decisions where most financial consequences originate. It enables self-enforcement, reducing dependence on supervision and lowering governance friction. Decisions move faster without sacrificing responsibility because judgment is already aligned with organizational priorities. Most importantly, culture endures. While policies can be rewritten and leaders replaced, deeply embedded norms sustain discipline across transitions.

Controls create fences. Culture creates gravity.

Leadership as the Cultural Engine

Culture does not diffuse evenly across an organization. It radiates from authority. People do not study policy manuals to understand financial discipline. They watch how leaders travel, hire, approve, spend, prioritize, and respond under pressure. Signals travel faster than memos. What leaders normalize becomes institutional behavior. Financial discipline, therefore, is not installed. It is modeled.

Founders:

Long before systems mature, founder behavior sets financial gravity. Early choices where to spend, where to wait, when to say no become reference stories repeated for years. These stories harden into institutional memory and quietly define acceptable conduct. Visible restraint carries symbolic weight. Modest offices, careful hiring, thoughtful capital deployment, these actions communicate stewardship more credibly than formal directives. They frame discipline as purpose-driven rather than cost-driven. At this stage, legitimacy comes less from position and more from example.

Moral authority travels further than hierarchy.

When founders treat capital as entrusted rather than available, discipline becomes a value rather than a rule.

CEOs:

As organizations scale, culture follows executive attention.

- What leaders review becomes what managers manage.
- What leaders question becomes what teams prepare for.
- What leaders tolerate becomes institutional permission.

Dashboards are not neutral; they are cultural instruments. Metrics signal priorities. If efficiency, returns, and capital productivity are consistently examined, discipline becomes part of performance identity. Moments of pressure are even more instructive. Market shocks, revenue shortfalls, and cost stress compress decision time and reveal true priorities. Structured responses reinforce discipline as a principle. Reactive decisions legitimize expediency. Even how trade-offs are framed teaches decision logic. When investment choices are discussed in terms of long-term value versus short-term optics, organizations learn how to think, not just what to decide.

The C-Suite:

If CEOs set a tone, the executive team scales it.

Each role translates discipline into its operational language:

- Finance leaders design the architecture, planning systems, capital-allocation logic, and performance metrics that turn stewardship into structure.
- Operations leaders convert discipline into habit through execution rhythms, efficiency standards, and process rigor.

- Commercial leaders shape the quality of growth through pricing integrity, return-on-investment discipline, and customer economics.

Culture strengthens when these signals converge. It fractures when they conflict.

Boards:

At the highest level, discipline is shaped by what is measured and what is rewarded. Board attention cascades. Discussion agendas influence executive focus, which shapes managerial priorities. Measurement focus becomes organizational focus. Compensation systems amplify this effect. Incentives encode values into economics. What gets rewarded gets repeated. When rewards favor sustainable value, capital efficiency, and disciplined growth, stewardship becomes rational rather than rhetorical. Oversight tone matters as well. Constructive challenge strengthens accountability. Performative scrutiny weakens it. Governance style influences whether discipline feels enabling or punitive.

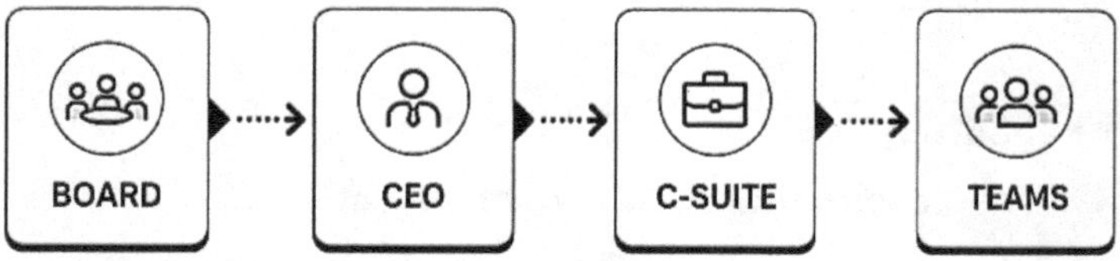

Leadership Influence Cascade

Cultural signals are strengthened by congruence across all levels of leadership. Financial discipline can only occur when there is coherence between what gets emphasized at the upper echelon of management and what actually happens throughout the organization.

When the emphases of governance priorities, executive behavior, managerial expectations, and performance systems are aligned, the discipline associated with financial discipline is consistent and sustainable.

Conversely, if any of these elements are inconsistent — for example, if the board emphasizes prudence while the executive leadership group celebrates obvious extravagance — the organization will send mixed messages about what constitutes acceptable behavior.

Sometimes leaders speak of using restraint but personally indulge to the fullest. Consequently, the values they articulate lose their legitimacy and credibility to the rank-and-file employees. If performance metrics focus on driving efficiency but career advancement promotes expansion at the cost of profits, the discipline associated with financial discipline gradually gives way to opportunism.

It is very rare for inconsistencies such as those described above to produce open conflict. Rather, such inconsistencies create considerable confusion among employees. Employees will tend to follow those cultural signals they perceive as having the greatest consequence, and will frequently place a higher priority on informal rewards than on formal principles. Over time, such cultural drift will cause employees to begin to fragment their organizational culture, dilute responsibility for holding one another accountable, and ultimately erode the behavioral norms necessary to sustain financial discipline.

People resolve contradictions by trusting behavior over messaging. The sequence is predictable:

1. Signals conflict
2. Trust declines
3. Informal rules emerge
4. Politics replaces performance
5. Discipline becomes optional

Culture then follows incentives, not intentions. Financial discipline cannot survive symbolic leadership. It requires behavioral coherence.

Everyday Behaviors That Build Discipline

A culture can last over time only if it is acted upon regularly. The financial policies/reviews alone will not provide ongoing motivation for financial discipline; it is the little things, repeated many times, that establish how activities in the organization get done. When stewardship is integrated into everyday routines, the expectation of being "disciplined" becomes a natural part of work.

At the day-to-day level, disciplined organizations develop simple yet impactful habits. A value-first filter is used to make decisions, where the primary question is not whether or not to do something, but rather whether it creates meaningful economic value, thereby changing the direction of the conversation from activity-oriented discussions to impact-oriented discussions and encouraging teams to consider the benefits compared to the resource commitment before they pursue an action.

Having visibility into spending is critical. When teams are aware of how their resources are being used, they can see the financial implications of their operational choices. The increased transparency reduces any impulse decision-making and encourages thoughtful prioritization. Finally, having visibility into spending reinforces that every time you spend money, you are making a trade-off.

Now, a critical factor is how one thinks about ownership. A steward will make decisions about resources given to them, rather than just a temporary employee with a budget. This type of consideration can lead to marginal changes in behavior, motivating careful commitments, conservative trade-offs, and responsible outcomes.

In addition to daily behaviors, disciplined organizations have recurring rituals that foster alignment and create learning opportunities.

For example, spending previews helps encourage discipline for future commitments before accumulation occurs.

Return-on-investment retrospectives provide a structured opportunity to evaluate whether past decisions delivered the expected value, ultimately fostering learning. The clarity on the financial runway helps create an understanding of capacity and limitations within the teams, thereby aligning ambition with sustainability. Associating efficiency with rewards reinforces that the disciplined execution of work is recognized as a value, not simply as a requirement of a disciplined environment.

Financial Discipline Operating Rhythms		
Frequency	**Ritual**	**Purpose**
Daily	Spend awareness	Reinforces micro-discipline in routine decisions
Weekly	ROI reviews	Creates continuous learning loops
Monthly	Runway alignment	Maintains strategic financial visibility
Quarterly	Zero-based resets	Strengthens structural efficiency

Language also shapes behavior. Disciplined cultures gradually replace reactive vocabulary with stewardship-oriented thinking. Conversations shift from blame to learning, encouraging reflection rather than defensiveness. Dependence on approvals gives way to ownership, empowering individuals to act responsibly without excessive gatekeeping. Restrictions are reframed as stewardship, emphasizing purposeful use of resources rather than constraints.

Through repeated routines and reinforcing language, financial discipline becomes embedded in the organization's thinking, decision-making, and day-to-day operations.

Building a Speak-Up Financial Culture

When weaknesses in financial discipline go unaddressed, the consequences can be severe. Common weak points associated with financial discipline include minor issues that develop into major crises if not resolved in time, incorrectly priced contracts, cost overruns, delays in collecting receivables, and unrealistic budget pressures. The initial development of these problems generally occurs within a related time frame and therefore does not appear to be a major problem. The extended period during which an individual hesitates to report a concern to a leader results in erosion of discipline. Consequently, a well-disciplined organization views the prompt escalation of financial issues not as a disagreement but as proper financial stewardship.

The reasons that lead to financial problems being hidden for a long period of time can be predicted. The most common barrier to reporting a concern is fear. People fear being perceived as incompetent, negative, or as resisting the momentum by raising a concern. In a high-performance organization where confidence is rewarded, the fear of damaging one's reputation can lead to significant silence about reporting certain issues. Over an extended period of time, structural silence may take hold within an organization: rigid reporting lines develop, upward communication is discouraged by hierarchy, and bad news passes through a filtration system and reaches decision-makers more slowly. Because of this extended period of time without reporting issues, the financial risk accumulates invisibly.

The development of psychological safety within the workplace creates a financial safety net. When employees can freely report a concern without fear of being blamed or retaliated against, the concern is reported earlier and addressed at a lower cost. Leaders are pivotal in creating this safety. They set the tone for an organization by how they respond to difficult information from employees.

When leaders acknowledge and support the early identification of concerns, responsible disclosure becomes commonplace. When uncomfortable truths are accepted rather than resisted, the organization becomes more transparent.

Disciplined organizations also normalize bad news as part of operational reality. Variances, misses, and emerging risks are treated as inputs for better decisions rather than triggers for fault-finding. Public learning loops, in which teams review setbacks, extract lessons, and adjust processes, reinforce the message that transparency improves performance. Over time, escalation shifts from being a personal risk to an institutional contribution.

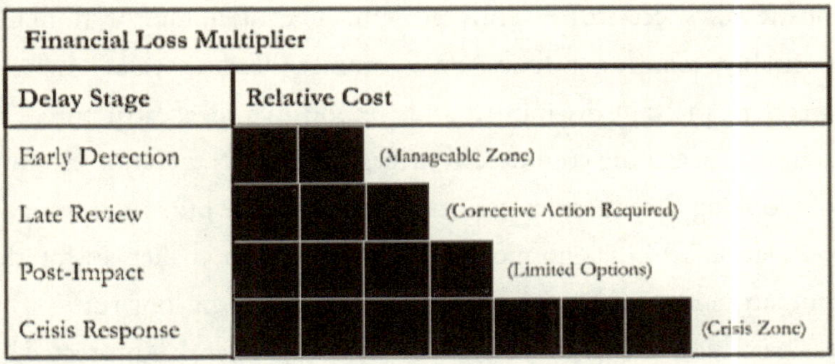

Structural mechanisms further reinforce a culture of speaking up. Safe reporting channels allow concerns to surface without procedural friction or political exposure. Skip-level escalation paths ensure that issues can bypass bottlenecks when necessary. Leadership vulnerability rituals, such as openly discussing mistakes, revisiting assumptions, and inviting challenges, signal that transparency is valued at the highest levels.

In financially disciplined organizations, speaking up is not an act of courage. It is an expected expression of stewardship.

Culture Across Functions

Only by embedding financial discipline across operating roles can it be made sustainable. Culture shouldn't be centrally driven by policies or specialist teams, but should manifest in the priorities and decisions of each department. Each function influences how resources are committed, protected, and converted into value. Therefore, when stewardship is viewed through functional responsibilities, the discipline will become an organizational capability rather than merely a procedural obligation. For example, in commercial teams, discipline originates with the definition of growth. Revenue volume is important, but revenue quality is just as important, so sales organizations need to consider both when determining what constitutes successful revenue growth. The discipline of thinking profitably requires a focus on customer lifetime value, margin integrity, pricing discipline, and responsible deal structure. In addition, measuring commercial success solely by transaction closings (not looking ahead) can create situations where the pursuit of revenue in isolation from economic considerations poses challenges for the company and can ultimately prove detrimental in the long run.

The value of an organization's supply chain network is protected by its procurement functions. The procurement function's responsibilities go beyond negotiating the best price for a product to include lifecycle value management. The manner in which vendors are selected, contracts are structured, demand is planned, and sourcing is applied determines whether the organization's spending translates into a long-term capability or an opportunity for waste. Organizational culture impacts how effectively these procurement functions deliver value to the organization by balancing cost savings against other factors (reliability, product quality, and the value of long-term partnership). Additionally, this type of culture serves to protect the organization from both visible expenses and invisible risks. Design decisions and operating efficiency will influence the way product and technology teams approach these disciplines.

As a result, decisions on architecture, development, infrastructure, and scalability will directly affect the organization's ability to manage its finances effectively. Efficiency within these areas is more than just technical excellence; it is about economic stewardship. Thoughtful design can reduce the need for rework, minimize complexity, and ensure that innovation can grow sustainably. When efficiency is seen as an indicator of excellence, it becomes part of the disciplined approach to building solutions.

Through policy design and standards for their use, human resources and administration will have a significant influence over the stewardship culture within the organization.

The manner in which employees are developed, supported, and compensated by their employer will drive the organization's ability to balance care and responsibility.

This focus on purpose, rather than perks, will help ensure that the organization's investments in its employees are directed toward building the capabilities, engagement, and performance of its workforce, rather than signaling indulgence. Administrative discipline will promote a fair, sustainable, and aligned approach to organizational priorities.

When each function interprets discipline through its own mandate, stewardship becomes distributed and self-reinforcing across the organization.

Functional Embedding Matrix		
Function	**Discipline Focus**	**Cultural Expression**
Sales	Profitable growth	Revenue quality, pricing integrity, and margin awareness
Procurement	Value protection	Cost efficiency, contract discipline, supplier stewardship
Product & Technology	Efficiency as excellence	Scalable design, resource-efficient architecture, sustainable innovation
HR & Administration	Purpose over perks	Responsible resource norms, capability-focused investment, and sustainable support systems

Incentives: The Real Culture Code

Their members' behaviors shape organizations. Although values can be established and communicated through written Codes of Conduct or other documents, values do not drive behavior. People will observe what gets rewarded, what gets ignored, and what can negatively affect an individual's career. It is through these observations that an organization creates its informal rules of conduct over time. Financial discipline is enhanced when strong stewardship of resources is viewed as rational (i.e., economical and professional), rather than merely ethical.

Performance management systems play a critical role in supporting this alignment of financial stewardship and behavior. Performance ratings that take into account both efficiency and effectiveness communicate that both quantity and quality of results are important.

Performance evaluations that measure how well an individual uses their resources (time, money, etc.) establish expectations for discipline in performance. Similarly, value-per-unit-of-resource metrics shift focus from the volume of activity performed to the economic return on invested resources, motivating teams to produce results that justify their costs.

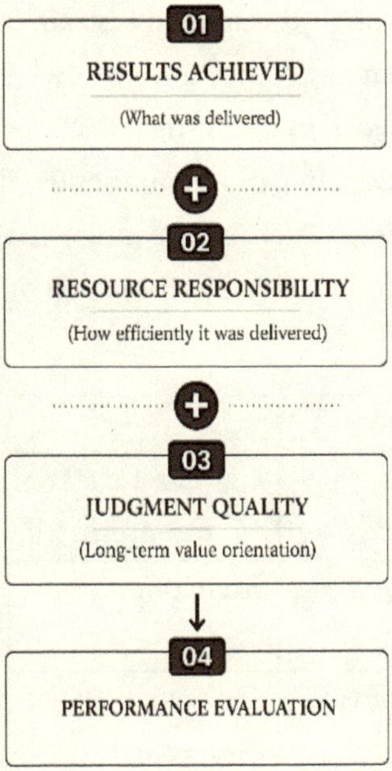

Promotion mechanisms also significantly impact the organization's culture. Promotion criteria provide employees with clarity about which behaviors and skills are associated with leadership and readiness to lead. When promotions are given to employees who demonstrate sound decision-making, responsible trade-offs, and a long-term value orientation, employees perceive a strong emphasis on discipline. Conversely, when promotions are granted based on factors such as visibility, activity volume, and short-term results, the signals associated with behavior will diminish in strength regardless of the organization's formal communications.

Performance Systems That Reinforce Discipline

Disciplined organizations design performance frameworks that integrate stewardship into evaluation criteria. Efficiency-weighted appraisals balance achievement with responsibility for resources. Metrics that examine value created per unit of investment strengthen economic thinking across roles.

Promotion pathways reinforce these expectations by recognizing leaders who combine ambition with prudence.

The Incentive Alignment Test

The strength of an organization's cultural code can be assessed through a simple test of consequences. What happens when an individual delivers meaningful savings through thoughtful restraint? How is visible overspending treated when outcomes are otherwise acceptable? When someone chooses prudence over prestige, declines unnecessary scale, defers symbolic expenditure, or recommends a smaller but wiser investment, does the system recognize the judgment involved? The answers reveal whether discipline is truly embedded or merely expressed.

The Incentive Alignment Test		
Situation	**If Discipline Is Real**	**If Culture Is Cosmetic**
Someone delivers meaningful savings	Recognized as value creation	Seen as under-ambition
Overspending is visible	Questioned regardless of outcome	Ignored if targets met
Prudence over prestige	Viewed as a leadership judgment	Viewed as a lack of boldness

Discipline, Trust, and Morale

Many people confuse financial discipline with being restrictive about what they can do. In fact, having a firm financial discipline creates a basis for trust. By showing people how you distribute resources, when you make trade-offs, and what constraints exist, uncertainty is reduced, and alignment is established.

By being clear about all these things, you create a common understanding of the organization's financial condition, the risks faced, and the priorities established for resources.

As a result of this common understanding, a common set of responsibilities develops.

When employees understand the economic environment in which they work, they make better decisions.

Part of trust is based on fairness. When times require restraint, employees closely monitor their leaders' actions. When leaders make sacrifices for the good of the organization and apply the same standards to themselves as they expect of their employees, their credibility is enhanced. Conversely, when the organization's disciplines are applied unevenly, employee morale is diminished, and employees see that you are managing them through control rather than care. In this sense, discipline is an asset — it protects the organization's resilience during a downturn, prevents it from losing strategic flexibility, and reduces the likelihood of having to take significant corrective actions. Having clear boundaries in place reduces the risk of overages due to poor planning and provides the organization with confidence that long-term growth is achievable. Disciplinary norms do not restrict organizations from pursuing their aspirations; they provide stability, enabling organizations to invest in opportunities responsibly.

Culture When Under Financial Stress

Downturns offer a clear view of an organization's culture. Financial stress is a true test of the structural vs. situational nature of discipline in an organization. During downturns, transparency contributes to stability, whereas secrecy can create instability. By openly discussing challenges, trade-offs, and recovery plans, the organization reduces speculation and builds trust.

The response patterns also influence the organization in a downturn. Disciplined organizations will work collaboratively to solve problems, rather than departmentalize them. Functions will work together to achieve enterprise priorities, rather than maintain departmental metrics. When one business unit faces constraints, the likelihood that it and other business units will coordinate their actions increases, thereby strengthening institutions.

Constraints themselves can serve as organizing mechanisms. They set clear boundaries that direct focus, clarify priorities, and reduce non-value-adding activity. Financial stress can increase alignment and reinforce the habits necessary to sustain long-term resilience if managed effectively.

Cautionary Patterns & Leadership Signals

Financial discipline typically does not break down quickly. Most likely, this occurs gradually over time through increasingly changing-styled and signaling conditions. For example, one way this can happen is when your personal or work lifestyle choice increases due to funding events or success. Increasing your visible discretionary expenditure can thus reset and normalize expectations that lead to excess.

Another way this can occur is when growth provides reasoning for not adhering to a standard of discipline. The "growth at all costs" type of stories often fail to take into account deteriorations in unit economics, which creates a weaker relationship between growth and corresponding value.

Metric theatre provides a stealthier type of risk. When report metrics emphasize presentation over fact, performance is less visible, and accountability is diminished. Therefore, appearances become more important than results.

Finally, when discipline relies primarily on individual vigilance rather than an organization's infrastructure, it can create fragility in the system. Organizations with strong cultures are sustainable because of their systems, not because of the individual personality.

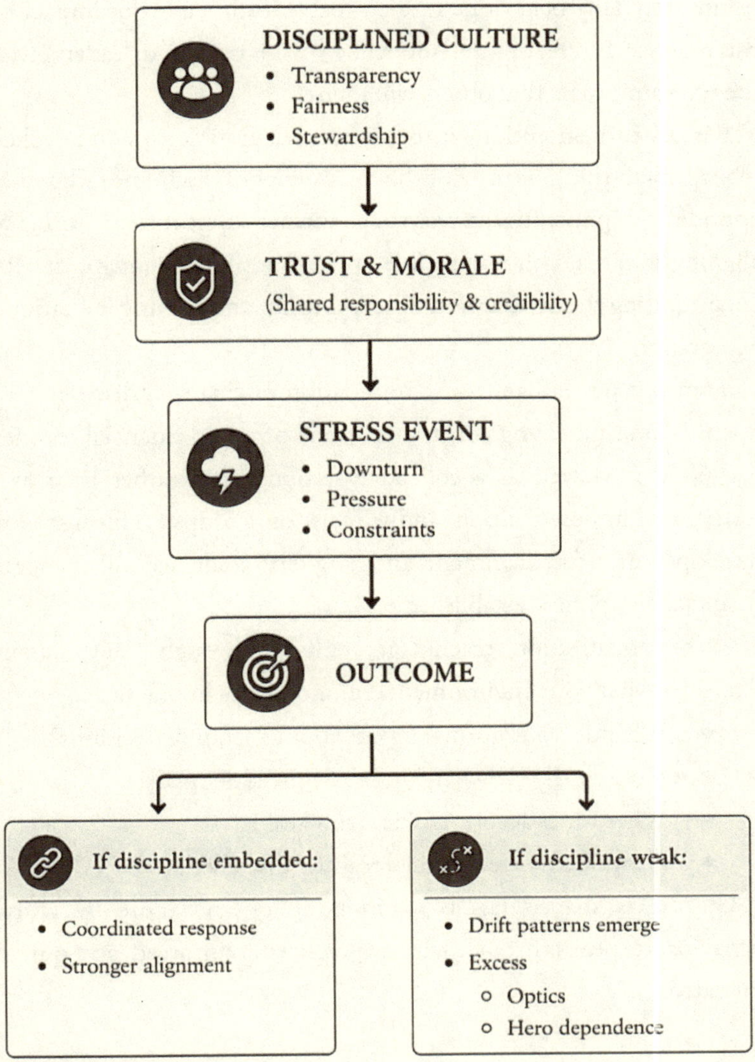

Controls are not the only sustaining mechanism for financial discipline; rather, they are supported by a cultural infrastructure that provides meaning to decisions throughout an organization. While systems and policies provide structure, stewardship is upheld by shared norms and daily behaviors. Leaders' behavior has a major impact on this practice. By creating and modeling what is rewarded, leaders create the economic logic that others will follow.

Rituals turn intentions into routines; daily practices and cyclical management rhythms provide the consistency of discipline rather than episodic discipline. Incentive systems further support these norms by aligning rewards with responsible or irresponsible judgment, thereby enculturating the expectation of stewardship and making it a rational expectation.

Transparency enhances the foundation of financial discipline; by openly communicating constraints, trade-offs, and financial realities, discipline is viewed as a collective responsibility rather than as a restriction imposed upon individuals or groups. Through this development, trust, alignment, and long-term resilience will emerge as financial discipline is established.

Every organization teaches its culture through daily signals. Consider what your environment communicates in practice:

- What do your norms suggest about spending decisions?
- How clearly is ownership of resources defined?
- Where does accountability truly reside?
- How openly are financial realities discussed?

Culture is shaped less by written policy and more by visible behavior. It speaks through what is practiced, reinforced, and quietly tolerated.

8

SYSTEMS, TOOLS & PRACTICES

Even the strongest intent toward financial discipline eventually runs into a hard reality: intent does not scale on its own. Organizations may begin with clarity, urgency, and even alignment around disciplined behavior, but without structure, that clarity fades. Decisions become inconsistent, exceptions increase, and over time, what once felt like discipline begins to look like discretion. The challenge is not in defining what good financial behavior looks like, but in sustaining it across people, time, and pressure.

This is where most organizations make a critical misstep. They recognize the need for structure, but interpret it as a need for systems that record activity rather than systems that shape behavior. They invest in automation, dashboards, and reporting layers, believing that visibility will naturally translate into control. But as seen repeatedly, visibility without enforcement does not create discipline; it simply makes indiscipline easier to observe. The result is a paradox: more data, more tools, more reporting, and yet, the same underlying behavior persists.

At the same time, culture alone is not enough. Many organizations pride themselves on having strong values, responsible teams, and leadership intent focused on discipline.

But culture, when left unsupported, becomes uneven in practice. Different teams interpret standards differently. Decision-making varies by individual. What is acceptable in one context becomes an exception in another. Over time, culture without structure creates pockets of discipline rather than a system of discipline.

Financial Discipline Organizations resolve this tension by clarifying the relationship between behavior and structure. If culture defines the intent the organization believes in and aspires to, then systems define the consistency with which that intent is applied in reality. In this sense, systems are not neutral tools. They are mechanisms that enforce boundaries, introduce friction where needed, and make consequences visible. They do not just record decisions; they shape them.

Without this structural backbone, even the most disciplined organizations begin to drift. Not because people lack intent, but because there is no consistent mechanism to reinforce it. Decisions get faster, but not better. Exceptions become easier, but less visible. Accountability weakens, not through neglect, but through inconsistency. The absence of structure does not create freedom; it creates variability.

This chapter explores that missing layer. Not systems as automation engines, but systems as discipline enforcers. Not tools that make processes faster, but tools that make behavior better. Because ultimately, financial discipline is not sustained by intention alone. It is sustained when systems are designed to make the right behavior the easiest path and the wrong behavior difficult, visible, and accountable.

The Seductive Appeal of Automation

Organizations rarely set out to weaken their financial discipline. In most cases, they invest heavily in systems, tools, and technologies to improve financial performance. Yet, despite these investments, many organizations find that discipline does not improve in proportion to the sophistication of their systems. This disconnect reflects a deeper issue: systems are often designed to automate activity, not to enforce disciplined behavior.

The appeal of automation is understandable. It is tangible, measurable, and easy to communicate. System implementations have defined timelines, clear deliverables, and visible outputs. Leadership teams can point to faster closing cycles, increased transaction volumes, and reduced manual effort as evidence of progress. Metrics such as invoices processed, reports generated, or workflows completed provide a sense of momentum. In this way, automation creates the appearance of control and advancement, even when underlying decision quality remains unchanged.

Equally important, automation is often the path of least resistance. Automating existing processes allows organizations to improve efficiency without fundamentally challenging how decisions are made. It does not require revisiting spending behaviors, redefining accountability, or questioning entrenched practices. Power structures remain intact, and financial responsibility can continue to be concentrated within the finance function rather than distributed across the organization. In this sense, automation enables change without disruption, preserving the status quo while signaling progress.

However, this approach carries high hidden costs. When organizations automate without first establishing discipline, they risk amplifying existing weaknesses. Inefficient or poorly governed processes, when executed faster, do not become better; they become more deeply embedded. Workarounds that once existed informally can become codified within systems. Over time, the organization may build increasingly complex structures to accommodate behaviors that were never aligned with disciplined financial management.

Dysfunction does not disappear; it becomes systematized.

Enabling financial discipline is inherently more demanding. It requires organizations to examine how decisions are made, how resources are allocated, and how accountability is enforced. This process often surfaces uncomfortable questions about spending patterns, risk acceptance, and leadership behavior. It demands commitment that extends beyond system implementation cycles and into the organization's ongoing practices. Unlike automation, which produces immediate and visible outputs, discipline develops gradually through consistent reinforcement.

The results of discipline are also less immediate and less easily attributed. Improvements emerge over time as behaviors change, processes align, and decision quality strengthens. The benefits compound, appearing not as a single transformation event but as a steady increase in resilience, predictability, and financial performance. In environments driven by short-term results, this slower progression can make discipline more difficult to prioritize.

At its core, the distinction is clear. Automation addresses symptoms; discipline addresses root causes. Organizations often choose automation because it is easier to implement systems than to reshape behavior. Yet sustainable financial performance depends not on how efficiently transactions are processed, but on how consistently sound decisions are made. Systems create value only when they reinforce this consistency by making disciplined behavior the default and rendering undisciplined behavior difficult to sustain.

Automation or Financial Discipline	
Automation Focus	**Discipline Enablement**
Activity efficiency	Decision quality
Transaction speed	Behavioral consistency
System outputs	Economic outcomes

Short-term ROI	Long-term resilience
Visible progress	Compounding impact

What Makes a System Truly Financial Discipline-Supporting

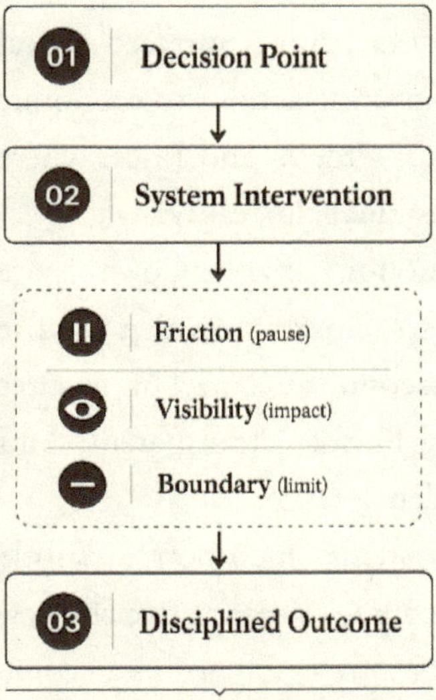

Where Discipline Happens

If systems are to serve financial discipline rather than merely record activity, their design must extend beyond efficiency. A discipline-supporting system is not defined by how quickly it processes transactions, but by how effectively it shapes decisions. In contrast to automation-first approaches, which prioritize speed and volume, FDO-aligned systems are structured to influence behavior at the point where financial choices are made.

The first defining characteristic is a shift from detection to prevention. Traditional systems identify issues after they occur, relying on reviews and reporting cycles to surface problems. Financial discipline-supporting systems intervene earlier. They are designed to block non-compliant actions before commitment, ensuring that financial discipline is embedded in execution rather than evaluated retrospectively. In this way, controls move from observation to enforcement.

Equally important is the intentional use of friction. While efficiency is often treated as the primary goal of system design, financially disciplined organizations recognize that certain decisions should not be frictionless. Introducing structured pauses at key thresholds forces evaluation, justification, and alignment with financial priorities.

This aligns with the broader principle that discipline requires consistent reinforcement through processes, not just oversight.

Visibility within these systems is also redefined. Rather than simply reporting outcomes, discipline-supporting systems make consequences explicit at the moment of decision. Financial trade-offs' impact on budgets, targets, or resource allocation is surfaced in real time, reinforcing accountability and connecting actions to economic outcomes. This reflects the integration of Process and Price, where operational decisions are directly linked to financial reality.

Boundaries within such systems are non-negotiable. Controls are not guidelines to be bypassed; they are structural limits that require formal escalation and visibility when exceptions occur. This ensures that deviations from discipline are deliberate, transparent, and accountable rather than informal or hidden.

At the behavioral level, these systems incorporate subtle reinforcement mechanisms. Defaults encourage conservative choices, comparisons provide context, and deviations from norms become visible. At the same time, accountability is preserved through clear ownership of decisions. Every action is traceable, reinforcing the principle that financial outcomes result from individual and collective choices.

Finally, financial disciplined systems simplify compliance. They make responsible behavior easier to execute than workarounds, aligning incentives with desired outcomes. When properly designed, the system itself guides behavior, making disciplined action the natural path. The defining test is straightforward: a discipline-supporting system makes good financial behavior easy, and poor behavior difficult, visible, and accountable. Only then does the system fulfill its role not as a recorder of activity, but as an enabler of discipline.

Designing Systems That Enforce Accountability

If discipline-supporting systems shape behavior at the point of decision, they must also ensure that accountability is not lost after the decision is made. Financial discipline is sustained when systems consistently reinforce four critical elements: clear decision logic, visible exception handling, traceable approvals, and controlled cash movement. These are not isolated controls but interconnected mechanisms that translate intent into enforceable practice.

The first requirement is to record the decision logic. Traditional systems capture outcomes approved or rejected, but rarely the reasoning behind them. In disciplined organizations, this is insufficient. Systems must require explicit articulation of *the rationale for* a decision before it is approved. This aligns with the broader principle that financial discipline depends on decision quality, not just process completion. When justification is structured and linked to strategic and economic considerations, it transforms approvals from procedural steps into accountable commitments. Over time, this creates a repository of decision patterns that reinforces consistent thinking across the organization.

Exception handling introduces a second layer of discipline. In policy-driven environments, exceptions often become routine, gradually eroding control. Discipline-supporting systems reverse this dynamic by making exceptions visible, deliberate, and consequential. Escalation mechanisms ensure that deviations are not contained within local decision loops but are exposed to broader organizational scrutiny. This reflects the cultural principle that financial outcomes are shared responsibilities. When exceptions require attention beyond immediate authority, they shift from being convenient workarounds to decisions that carry institutional visibility.

Approval tracking further strengthens this structure by embedding personal accountability. Systems must ensure that decisions are attributable to individuals rather than to processes. When approvals are traceable and consistently monitored, they reinforce the expectation that judgment cannot be delegated to systems. This aligns with the distinction established earlier: technology can structure workflows, but responsibility remains human. By making approval behavior visible over time, organizations create feedback loops that encourage consistency, prudence, and alignment with financial expectations.

The objective is not to create exhaustive documentation or restrictive oversight. It is to ensure that disciplined behavior becomes the natural outcome of system interaction. When systems make accountability unavoidable, visibility immediate, and circumvention difficult, they fulfill their role within a Financial Discipline Organization not as passive record-keepers, but as active enforcers of responsible decision-making.

Operating Rhythms That Sustain Financial Discipline

Financial discipline does not endure through isolated decisions or periodic reviews. It is sustained through consistent operating rhythms that embed visibility, accountability, and action into the organization's cadence. As established earlier, discipline emerges when behavior is reinforced continuously through systems, culture, and structured routines. These rhythms ensure that financial awareness is not episodic, but constant, and that decision-making remains aligned with economic reality at every level.

At the core of this structure are internal financial health reviews conducted at multiple frequencies. Each cadence serves a distinct purpose, collectively ensuring that no material shift in financial position goes unnoticed. At the daily level, focus remains narrow and immediate: cash position, critical payment alerts, and emerging red flags. These checks reinforce micro-discipline, ensuring that short-term liquidity and operational risks are actively monitored rather than assumed.

Weekly reviews expand the lens. Burn rate against plan, key variances, and updated cash runway provide a forward-looking view of financial stability. This cadence reflects the principle that discipline is not only about tracking outcomes but about anticipating deviation. By concentrating attention on a limited set of critical indicators, organizations maintain clarity without diluting focus.

Monthly reviews introduce a broader evaluation of performance. Full profit-and-loss assessments, departmental outcomes, and emerging trends create a structured opportunity to connect operational activity to financial results. This aligns with the integration of Process and Price, ensuring that execution is consistently evaluated against economic contribution.

Quarterly reviews further deepen this perspective, incorporating strategic alignment and preparing insights for governance forums. These cycles ensure that discipline is maintained not only in operations but also in long-term direction.

Complementing these reviews is a structured approach to scenario planning and financial buffers. Discipline requires preparedness for variability, not just control under stable conditions. Monthly scenario updates, typically across base, best, and worst cases, ensure that assumptions remain current and that financial projections reflect evolving realities. These updates reinforce adaptability without sacrificing structure.

Quarterly stress testing extends this thinking by examining structural resilience. By explicitly identifying potential disruptors to the organization and evaluating the adequacy of existing buffers, leadership teams reinforce the principle that discipline includes anticipating downside risk. Annual planning consolidates these insights, aligning future scenarios, buffer targets, and contingency plans with strategic priorities. Across all cycles, the objective remains consistent: to ensure that financial capacity is understood, protected, and deliberately managed.

Buffers themselves require regular validation. Cash runway and operating flexibility are not static measures but dynamic indicators of resilience. Periodic assessment ensures that thresholds remain meaningful and that early warning signals are acted upon before constraints become critical. This reflects the broader FDO principle that discipline is proactive rather than reactive.

Policy reviews and exception analysis provide reinforcement. As discussed earlier, discipline-supporting systems make exceptions visible and consequential. Structured review cadences ensure that these signals are not ignored.

Weekly scans identify immediate issues and emerging patterns, allowing for timely intervention. Monthly analysis deepens this review by focusing on root causes and determining whether deviations reflect isolated incidents or systemic weaknesses. Quarterly policy reviews extend beyond enforcement to evaluation. They assess whether existing rules continue to support disciplined behavior or whether they introduce unnecessary complexity. This aligns with the principle of simplicity in compliance, ensuring that systems make the right behavior easier rather than more burdensome. Annual resets consolidate these learnings, refining policies to remain clear, relevant, and aligned with organizational priorities.

The underlying principle is consistency. Discipline is not defined by perfect analysis or exhaustive control, but by the absence of surprise.

When organizations maintain steady visibility into their financial position, respond promptly to signals, and align decisions with structured rhythms, discipline becomes embedded in their operations. Over time, these routines transform financial management from a periodic activity into a continuous capability, one that sustains performance, reinforces accountability, and supports resilience across changing conditions.

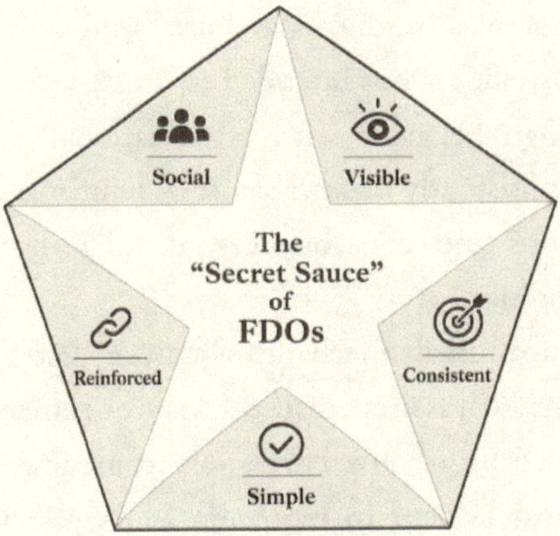

Institutionalizing Financial Discipline Through Practice

Financial discipline becomes durable only when it is translated from principle into repeated, visible behavior. As established in earlier chapters, culture is not defined by policy, but by what is consistently practiced, reinforced, and observed. Systems can enforce structure, and authority can define accountability, but discipline becomes institutionalized only when it is embedded into the everyday rhythms, interactions, and signals of the organization. One of the most effective ways to achieve this is through behavioral rituals. Structured forums that require teams to explain financial outcomes, particularly variances, transform abstract accountability into lived experience.

When deviations from plan are openly discussed, supported by facts, and followed by corrective action, discipline becomes a shared responsibility rather than a private exercise.

These rituals reinforce the principle that financial outcomes are collective, aligning with the distributed accountability central to Financial Discipline Organizations.

Visibility further strengthens this dynamic. When financial performance is transparent across teams, it fosters a shared understanding of how resources are used and where discipline is applied. This visibility is not intended to create pressure for its own sake, but to align behavior with organizational priorities. When outcomes are consistently observable, they reinforce the connection between decisions and consequences, making discipline tangible rather than theoretical.

Cultural reinforcement mechanisms ensure that these signals are sustained. Norms such as immediate disclosure of emerging issues shift the organization from reactive correction to proactive management. Discipline is most evident in moments when policy is silent, and judgment takes over. Encouraging early reporting of risks or deviations ensures that problems are addressed before they escalate, reinforcing both transparency and trust. Recognition systems further support this culture by highlighting responsible behavior. When prudent decision-making and efficient resource use are acknowledged, discipline becomes not only expected but valued.

Process integration extends these principles into decision-making itself.

By requiring structured evaluation of potential risks before committing resources, organizations reinforce the expectation that financial decisions must be deliberate and informed. Similarly, ongoing evaluation of external relationships, such as vendor performance, ensures that spending translates into sustained value rather than passive cost accumulation.

These practices align with the broader FDO principle that discipline must be embedded across all functions and decisions, not confined to isolated controls.

Leadership behavior remains central to institutionalization. As emphasized in prior chapters, culture radiates from authority. When leaders demonstrate transparency in their own financial decisions, adhere to the same standards expected of others, and participate visibly in financial discussions, they reinforce the legitimacy of discipline. Consistency between what is communicated and what is practiced is essential. Where leadership behavior aligns with stated principles, discipline strengthens; where it diverges, credibility erodes.

Across all these practices, a consistent pattern emerges. Financial discipline becomes institutionalized when it is social, visible, reinforced, simple, and consistent. Social reinforcement ensures that expectations are upheld not only by leadership but by peers. Visibility ensures that behavior is observable and aligned. Reinforcement ensures that discipline is recognized and sustained. Simplicity ensures that processes are followed rather than bypassed. Consistency ensures that discipline applies uniformly, without exception.

The ultimate measure of institutionalization is clarity. When a new member of the organization can quickly understand how financial decisions are made, how accountability is enforced, and how behavior is evaluated, discipline has moved beyond policy into culture.

At that point, it no longer depends on supervision or intervention. It becomes the organization's default way of operating, embedded, reinforced, and sustained through everyday practice.

The Core Test: *Is Discipline Real or System-Dependent?*

Ask these Questions:

- Does behavior persist without tools?
- Are decisions driven by logic or workflow?
- Is accountability cultural or system-enforced?

Your answers will tell you how to proceed further.

When Systems Replace Discipline

The pattern is consistent across organizations: significant investments in financial systems do not always translate into improved discipline. This disconnect emerges when technology is expected to create behavior rather than reinforce it. At the root of this failure is a belief that systems can act as a "magic button" delivering immediate transformation without requiring corresponding changes in accountability, decision-making, or culture.

In such environments, leadership often assumes that implementing sophisticated tools will automatically establish control. This assumption leads to minimal investment in behavioral alignment. When expected improvements fail to materialize, frustration is directed at the system rather than at the underlying absence of discipline. The result is a cycle of replacement rather than resolution.

One visible outcome of this approach is the emergence of what can be described as compliance without impact. Organizations produce detailed dashboards, extensive procedures, and structured workflows, yet these elements remain disconnected from actual decision-making. Information is available, but not acted upon. Processes are defined, but not followed. Control appears strong from a structural perspective, yet behavior remains unchanged.

Over time, this misalignment becomes most evident in the treatment of exceptions. Initially, systems are designed assuming that deviations will be rare. However, in the absence of embedded discipline, exceptions gradually increase. What begins as a controlled mechanism for handling unique cases evolves into a routine pathway for bypassing controls. Eventually, the exception becomes indistinguishable from the standard process, undermining the very purpose of the system.

In contrast, organizations that prioritize behavior before systems demonstrate a different trajectory. Discipline is first established through simple, transparent practices often without reliance on complex tools. Decision-making is made visible, accountability is reinforced, and habits are built through repetition. Only after these patterns are stable are systems introduced to scale them. In such cases, technology enhances consistency rather than compensating for its absence.

The distinction between these approaches highlights a central principle: discipline is not created through complexity. It is built through clarity, consistency, and reinforcement. When systems are introduced into environments where these elements are already present, they strengthen discipline. When introduced in their absence, they create the appearance of control while masking underlying weaknesses.

The implication is clear. Financial discipline cannot be digitized into existence. It must be established through behavior and then supported by systems. Without this foundation, even the most advanced tools remain disconnected from the outcomes they are intended to improve.

Choosing Tools That Reinforce Discipline

If systems are to support financial discipline effectively, they must align with the organization's current maturity level. As outlined in earlier chapters, discipline progresses from fragmented practices to an integrated capability. Tool selection must therefore reflect this progression, ensuring that complexity is introduced only when behavior is ready to sustain it.

Organizations in the early stages of a discipline benefit from simplicity. Basic tools that provide visibility and reinforce accountability are often sufficient. As discipline strengthens, systems can expand to support scale, integration, and consistency. Attempting to implement advanced solutions before foundational practices are established leads to misalignment, low adoption, and increased workarounds.

The most common error is premature complexity. Organizations adopt comprehensive systems designed for mature environments, then struggle to integrate them into existing practices. This reflects a reversal of the natural progression of discipline, introducing structure before behavior is ready to operate within it. As discussed earlier, this leads to partial usage, fragmented processes, and reliance on informal alternatives.

Effective tool selection, therefore, begins with clarity of purpose. Rather than attempting to address multiple challenges simultaneously, organizations should focus on specific areas where discipline needs reinforcement. Tools should be evaluated based on their ability to simplify and strengthen behavior, not on the breadth of their features.

Three criteria provide a practical guide. First, the tool must make disciplined behavior easier to execute than non-compliance. Second, it should reinforce visibility and accountability, enabling teams to understand and act on financial signals.

Third, it must surface issues promptly, supporting the operating rhythms that sustain discipline. Tools that fail to meet these criteria risk becoming additional layers of complexity rather than enablers of control. Equally important are indicators of misalignment.

Systems that require extensive implementation, generate excessive reporting, or demand prolonged training often signal overengineering. When tools are difficult to use or understand, they discourage adoption and encourage circumvention. This undermines the earlier-established principle of simplicity, which holds that disciplined behavior must be the path of least resistance. A more effective approach follows a staged progression. Organizations begin with simple methods, refine them through practice, and gradually introduce tools that codify what works. This ensures that systems reflect actual behavior rather than theoretical design. Over time, this alignment enables scalability without sacrificing discipline.

Ultimately, the role of technology within a Financial Discipline Organization is not to define how decisions are made, but to reinforce how they are already made. Tools should remain proportional to the organization's needs, supporting clarity, consistency, and accountability without introducing unnecessary complexity. When this alignment is achieved, systems become enablers of discipline rather than obstacles to it.

Two Paths to Financial Discipline	
Behavior-First	**Tool-First**
Build habits first	Buy the system first.
Add tools later	Force-fit behavior
High adoption	Low adoption
Sustained discipline	Temporary control

The Limits of Systems: What ERPs Cannot Do

While systems play a critical role in reinforcing discipline, their limitations must be clearly understood. The misconception that technology creates control often leads to over-reliance on systems, particularly enterprise platforms. These systems are highly effective in certain domains, but they are frequently expected to perform functions that lie beyond their design.

At their core, systems are designed to record, structure, and standardize transactions. They provide consistency in execution, enforce defined workflows, and generate reports that reflect financial activity. These capabilities are essential for scale and compliance. However, they operate within predefined rules and historical data, which limits their ability to address the dynamic and judgment-driven aspects of financial discipline.

One of the most common misconceptions is that systems can make decisions. In reality, they can only present information. Variances, trends, and anomalies can be identified, but the interpretation of these signals and the actions required remains the responsibility of individuals. This reflects a broader principle established throughout the chapter: discipline is rooted in the quality of decisions, not in data availability.

Similarly, systems cannot anticipate all risks. They track commitments and record transactions, but they do not capture the full context in which financial outcomes unfold. External factors, behavioral patterns, and emerging risks often fall outside the scope of structured data. As a result, reliance on systems alone can create a false sense of security, where visibility is mistaken for control.

Another limitation lies in the system's inability to assess relationships and intent. Controls can verify compliance with rules, but they cannot evaluate the underlying motivations or connections that may influence decisions. This reinforces the need for accountability structures and cultural reinforcement. Without these elements, systems remain vulnerable to manipulation within the boundaries they enforce.

Context presents an additional challenge. Financial data does not exist in isolation; it reflects underlying business activity, strategic choices, and external conditions. Systems can highlight deviations, but they cannot interpret whether those deviations are justified. This requires human judgment, informed by both financial and operational understanding.

Perhaps most critically, systems cannot change behavior. They can log violations, enforce steps, and provide visibility, but they cannot replace the conversations, expectations, and consequences that drive discipline. As established in Chapter 7, culture is built through leadership behavior and consistent reinforcement. Systems support this process, but they do not initiate it.

The same limitation applies to accountability. Distributing information widely does not ensure ownership. Reports may be accessible to many, but responsibility must be clearly defined and consistently enforced. Without this clarity, systems risk creating diffusion rather than accountability.

Systems are inherently retrospective. They analyze what has occurred, not what could occur. While they provide valuable insight into past performance, they cannot fully anticipate future conditions or replace forward-looking judgment. This distinction reinforces the role of scenario planning and operating rhythms in sustaining discipline.

Understanding these limitations clarifies the appropriate role of systems within a Financial Discipline Organization.

They are tools for consistency, visibility, and scale, not substitutes for leadership, judgment, or culture. When organizations expect systems to perform beyond these capabilities, they risk misalignment and over-reliance.

The distinction can be summarized. Systems can record, enforce, and report. They cannot think, judge, adapt, or care. Financial discipline emerges from the latter.

When this balance is understood, technology becomes a powerful enabler. When it is misunderstood, it becomes a source of false confidence.

<table>
<tr><td colspan="2">1. Make Decisions</td></tr>
<tr><td>ERP Says: "Budget variance -23%"</td><td>You need: "Fire vendor or renegotiate?"</td></tr>
<tr><td colspan="2">Reality: ERPs show problems; humans solve them</td></tr>
<tr><td colspan="2">2. Predict Cash Crises</td></tr>
<tr><td>ERP Shows: "AR: $2M, AP: $1M, all good."</td><td>Reality: Customer is bankrupt, bills due tomorrow</td></tr>
<tr><td colspan="2">Truth: ERPs track promises, not cash</td></tr>
<tr><td colspan="2">3. Catch Smart Fraud</td></tr>
<tr><td>ERP: Approved! (within limits, proper coding)</td><td>Reality: Employee's spouse owns the vendor</td></tr>
<tr><td colspan="2">Lesson: ERPs check rules, not relationships</td></tr>
<tr><td colspan="2">4. Understand Context</td></tr>
<tr><td>ERP: "Travel up 300%!"</td><td>Context: Landed the biggest client ever</td></tr>
<tr><td colspan="2">Problem: ERPs can't read the room</td></tr>
</table>

<table>
<tr><td colspan="2">5. Fix Bad Behavior</td></tr>
<tr><td>ERP: "Policy violation logged."</td><td>Needed: Uncomfortable conversation</td></tr>
<tr><td colspan="2">Truth: Systems don't change culture, leaders do</td></tr>
<tr><td colspan="2">6. Replace Judgment</td></tr>
<tr><td>ERP: "Historical data suggests..."</td><td>Reality: "But this time is different because..."</td></tr>
<tr><td colspan="2">Fact: ERPs analyze the past; you navigate the future</td></tr>
<tr><td colspan="2">7. Create Accountability</td></tr>
<tr><td>ERP: "Report sent to 47 people."</td><td>Reality: No one feels responsible</td></tr>
<tr><td colspan="2">Fix: One throat to choke beats perfect distribution list</td></tr>
<tr><td colspan="2">8. Know What's Missing</td></tr>
<tr><td>ERP: "All transactions recorded."</td><td>Missing: The deal that didn't close</td></tr>
<tr><td colspan="2">Blind Spot: ERPs track what happened, not what didn't</td></tr>
<tr><td colspan="2">9. Build Trust</td></tr>
<tr><td>ERP: "Audit trail complete."</td><td>Trust: "I know he wouldn't do that."</td></tr>
<tr><td colspan="2">Reality: Character beats compliance</td></tr>
<tr><td colspan="2">10. Save a Dying Company</td></tr>
<tr><td>ERP: "Implemented new cash management module."</td><td>Needed: Cut 50% of costs yesterday</td></tr>
<tr><td colspan="2">Truth: ERPs optimize process, not survival</td></tr>
</table>

The Human Multiplier in System Effectiveness

Across all previous sections, a consistent pattern emerges: systems do not determine outcomes, people do. Technology can enforce structure, enable visibility, and scale processes, but its effectiveness is ultimately shaped by how individuals engage with it. The same system, implemented in two different environments, can produce entirely different results. This variation is not driven by technical capability, but by human behavior.

At the core of this dynamic is ownership. In organizations where individuals view systems as mechanisms to avoid responsibility, tools become barriers rather than enablers. Processes are followed mechanically, often with the intent of transferring accountability to the system itself. In contrast, when individuals operate with an ownership mindset, systems are used to accelerate problem-solving and improve outcomes. The distinction is subtle but significant: one approach treats the system as a shield, the other as a tool.

Cultural context shapes how systems are experienced across the organization. In environments characterized by control and caution, systems tend to accumulate layers of approval and verification, increasing complexity and slowing decision-making. In contrast, cultures grounded in trust and accountability enable simpler, faster processes without compromising discipline. As established earlier, the number of controls does not define discipline; rather, it is the consistency of behavior that defines it. Systems must align with this principle to remain effective.

Incentives reinforce these behaviors. When performance is measured through activity rather than outcomes, systems are often used to satisfy requirements rather than to drive results. This can lead to distorted data, reduced reliability, and diminished trust in the system itself.

When incentives align with outcomes, individuals are more likely to engage meaningfully with tools, ensuring that the captured information reflects reality and supports decision-making.

Leadership behavior acts as the most significant multiplier. As emphasized throughout the chapter, culture is shaped by example. When leaders bypass systems or disregard established processes, it signals that discipline is optional.

This behavior cascades quickly, undermining the integrity of both systems and controls. Conversely, when leaders consistently engage with systems, rely on their outputs, and adhere to the same standards expected of others, they reinforce discipline across the organization. The impact of this alignment extends beyond individual actions, shaping collective behavior.

These factors, ownership, decision rights, capability, culture, incentives, and leadership, combine to determine the overall effectiveness of any system. Their influence is not additive, but multiplicative. Technical capability provides the foundation, but human behavior defines the outcome. Investments in systems without corresponding investments in these elements result in limited returns, regardless of the technology's sophistication.

The implication is clear. Organizations seeking to improve financial discipline must focus as much on people as on systems. Clarity of ownership, alignment of incentives, development of capability, and consistency of leadership behavior are not complementary to system design; they are foundational to it.

Without these elements, systems remain underutilized and ineffective. With them, systems become powerful enablers of disciplined, consistent, and scalable financial performance.

Why People Matter More Than Systems

System Value = Technical Capability × (People Factor)²

People Factor includes:

Ownership

Decision Rights

Capability

Culture

Leadership

₹10Cr system + fearful employees = ₹1Cr value

₹1Cr system + empowered owners = ₹100Cr value

The brutal truth: Companies spend 90% on systems, 10% on people readiness, then wonder why ROI is negative.

Impact of People on System Value	
Weak People Factor	**Strong People Factor**
Low adoption	High adoption
Workarounds	Alignment
Data entry	Decision-making
Bureaucracy	Enablement

A Practical FDO Toolkit Rules That Enforce Discipline

Financial discipline becomes real only when it is translated into clear, enforceable rules. As established throughout this chapter, systems alone cannot create discipline; they can only reinforce it. What organizations need, therefore, is not more tools, but a set of behavioral and operational rules that can be applied within existing systems or even without them.

These rules act as a practical toolkit, ensuring that discipline is consistently applied across people, processes, and decisions.

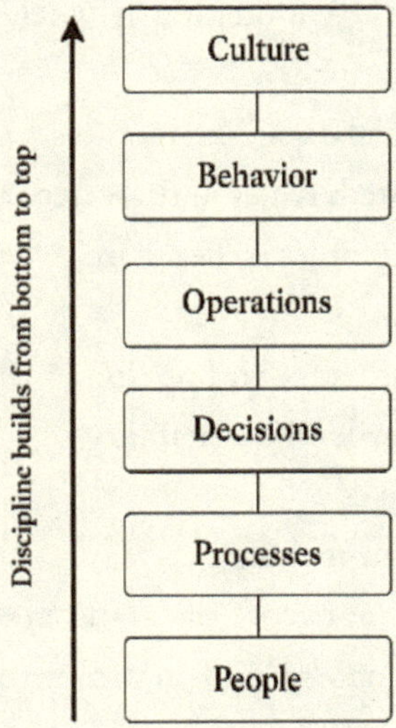

At its core, this toolkit is designed around a simple principle: make disciplined behavior the default, and indiscipline difficult, visible, and consequential.

1. People Rules: Financial discipline begins with people. Without ownership, systems become compliance mechanisms rather than decision enablers. Key rules include:

- Hiring for an ownership mindset rather than passive execution
- Establishing rapid feedback cycles instead of delayed evaluation
- Encouraging action without unnecessary permission layers
- Ensuring universal visibility into financial outcomes

These rules reinforce what earlier sections emphasized: accountability must be personal, not procedural. When individuals think and act like owners, discipline becomes intrinsic rather than enforced.

2. Process Rules: Processes often become the greatest source of friction and inefficiency. In FDOs, processes are designed not only for control but also for clarity and speed. Core rules include:

- Time-bound decision-making to prevent drift
- Simplification of communication and documentation

- Continuous elimination of redundant processes
- Limiting approval layers to maintain accountability

These rules align with earlier principles of friction by design: introducing friction where necessary but eliminating it when it creates delay without improving decision quality.

3. Price and Decision Rules: Financial discipline requires clarity in how value is created and evaluated. Rules in this category ensure that decisions are aligned with outcomes rather than assumptions. Key elements include:

- Transparency in financial performance and pricing
- Clear understanding of customer-level profitability
- Rapid response to external changes
- Emphasis on value-based decision-making

These rules reinforce the earlier concept of transparent consequences, in which decisions are evaluated based on their actual impact rather than their intent.

4. Operational Rules: Discipline must be visible to be sustained. Operational rules ensure that financial performance is continuously monitored and understood. Examples include:

- Daily visibility into financial performance
- Open sharing of mistakes and learnings
- Continuous benchmarking against higher standards
- Measurement of both speed and quality

These practices connect directly to earlier discussions on visibility and operating cadence. When performance is visible, accountability follows naturally.

5. Behavioral Rules: Discipline is not only about financial decisions, but it is reflected in how work is conducted day to day.

Behavioral rules shape how individuals interact with systems and with each other. These include:

- Driving decisions to closure within defined forums
- Encouraging direct, transparent communication
- Reducing unnecessary communication overhead
- Linking individual actions to financial outcomes

These rules reinforce the idea that discipline is not episodic; it is continuous and embedded in routine behavior.

6. Cultural Rules: Culture determines whether discipline persists over time. Rules in this category ensure that the organization consistently reinforces desired behavior. Core elements include:

- Open acknowledgment and learning from failures
- Elimination of informal or political decision-making
- Continuous learning and improvement
- Protection of sustainable work practices

As established earlier, culture is the ultimate enforcer of discipline. Systems can support it, but only culture can sustain it.

The effectiveness of this toolkit depends not on its completeness, but on its sequencing and consistency. Organizations should implement these rules in phases, beginning with foundational elements that establish ownership, visibility, and clarity of decision-making. A phased approach ensures:

- Early wins that reinforce behavior
- Gradual alignment across teams
- Reduced resistance to change
- Sustainable adoption over time

This aligns with the broader principle discussed throughout the chapter: discipline is built through repetition and reinforcement, not through one-time transformation. This toolkit is not about adding more rules; it is about creating the right rules. Each rule serves a specific purpose: to make disciplined behavior easier, faster, and more natural than indiscipline.

Across all categories, a consistent pattern emerges:

- Ownership replaces compliance
- Simplicity replaces complexity
- Visibility replaces ambiguity
- Action replaces delay

When these conditions are met, systems, whether simple or advanced, become effective enablers. Without them, even the most sophisticated tools remain underutilized.

Before implementing any rule, organizations should ask:

- Does this make disciplined behavior easier?
- Does it reinforce accountability?
- Does it increase visibility of outcomes?

If the answer is no, the rule adds complexity without strengthening discipline.

Financial Discipline Organizations are not defined by the tools they use, but by the rules they live by. Systems may vary, tools may evolve, but disciplined behavior once embedded remains consistent.

The goal is not to build perfect systems. It is to build consistent behavior so that systems can scale.

DISCIPLINE = OWNERSHIP + SIMPLICITY + VISIBILITY + CONSISTENCY

Discipline Equation

The Financial Discipline Readiness Test

Financial discipline cannot be imposed through systems, workflows, or even well-designed rules. It is a condition that must already exist at least in intent and leadership behavior before it can be scaled. Tools and frameworks do not create discipline; they expose the gap between what an organization claims to value and how it actually behaves. This is why many implementations fail quietly. The system works exactly as designed, but the organization does not.

Before introducing any new financial tool, workflow, or rule set, organizations must pause and ask a more fundamental question: *Are we ready to operate differently?* Not in theory, but in daily behavior.

Because once discipline is made visible through transparency, accountability, and enforced rules, it creates discomfort. It challenges habits, exposes inconsistencies, and redistributes power. If that discomfort is not anticipated and accepted, the organization will revert to old behaviors, often using the new system as a facade of progress.

1. **Leadership Readiness:** Every system reflects leadership behavior. Not intention, not communication, but behavior. If leaders bypass rules, make exceptions for themselves, or selectively enforce standards, the system immediately loses credibility. What follows is predictable: others begin to interpret rules as flexible, enforcement becomes inconsistent, and discipline erodes.

Category	Question	Why It Matters	Red Flag
Leadership Commitment	Will I personally follow every rule without exception?	Leadership behavior sets the ceiling for discipline	"Some rules won't apply to leadership."
Current Reality	What percentage of people will resist or leave?	Signals the depth of change required	"Minimal impact expected."
Power Structure	Who loses decision authority?	Resistance often hides in hierarchy	"Everyone agrees"

Sacred Practices	What existing behaviors will stop?	Tests real willingness to change	"We can keep most of what we do."

These questions are not theoretical; they are diagnostic. For example, if a leader believes that certain rules should not apply to senior management, the system will never enforce discipline. It will instead reinforce hierarchy. Similarly, underestimating resistance often indicates that the organization does not fully understand how deeply current behaviors are embedded. Discipline is not tested when rules are easy to follow; it is tested when they are inconvenient for leadership.

2. **Risk Readiness:** Introducing financial discipline, especially in organizations that have relied on flexibility or informal processes creates disruption. Decisions slow down initially, accountability increases, and previously hidden inefficiencies become visible. This can feel like regression, even though it is necessary progress.

Area	Critical Question	If Not Ready...	Required Action
Financial	Can we sustain disruption in execution?	Limited financial buffer	Strengthen liquidity first
Talent	Do we have enough ownership mindset today?	Low ownership density	Start with focus groups
Customer	Will changes impact experience?	High dependency on stability	Phase implementation
Competition	Can we retain empowered talent?	Weak positioning	Align incentives first
Regulatory	Do rules conflict with compliance?	High regulatory exposure	Validate constraints early

Organizations often underestimate this phase because they expect immediate efficiency gains. In reality, discipline introduces controlled friction, forcing better decisions at the cost of short-term speed. If the organization cannot absorb this friction, it will revert to faster, less disciplined behavior. Discipline compounds over time, but its early stages often feel like constraint rather than progress.

3. **Capability Readiness:** Even when intent and willingness exist, the organization must have the capability to function within a disciplined framework. This includes decision-making speed, clarity of communication, and the ability to operate transparently.

Dimension	Question	Minimum Expectation	If Not Ready...
Speed	Can decisions be made quickly and clearly?	Manual processes acceptable	Do not rely on systems
Transparency	Can financial performance be openly shared?	Willingness to show reality	Start with partial visibility
Trust	Can authority be distributed?	Limited but real delegation	Build gradually
Failure	Can leadership openly acknowledge mistakes?	A recent example exists	Delay transformation
Politics	Will performance outweigh informal influence?	Clear willingness	Address before scaling

For instance, if leadership is uncomfortable sharing real financial performance, including losses, then any system that increases visibility will be resisted. Similarly, if trust is low, attempts to distribute decision-making authority will lead to over-control or constant overrides. Systems cannot compensate for missing capabilities; they only magnify them.

4. **Rule-Level Validation:** Each rule introduced into the system must be evaluated not for its logic, but for its real-world consequences. A rule that appears sound in isolation may create unintended complexity or resistance when applied.

Rule Area	Key Question	Focus
Ownership	What is the cost of misaligned authority?	Define expectations clearly
Accountability	Can consequences be applied consistently?	Avoid selective enforcement
Autonomy	What risks increase with less control?	Ensure visibility mechanisms
Incentives	Can the financial impact be sustained?	Align with long-term outcomes.
Speed	Does faster decision-making reduce quality?	Start with reversible decisions.

The number of rules does not define discipline-supporting systems, but rather by how effectively those rules shape behavior.

5. **Cultural Readiness:** Culture is the most significant determinant of whether a discipline will sustain or collapse. It defines how people respond when rules are enforced, when transparency increases, and when accountability becomes visible.

Question	Self-Score (1–10)	Minimum
Comfort with visible failure		7
Ability to accept direct feedback		8
Willingness to reward initiative		9
Tolerance for independent decisions		6
Openness to challenge authority		7

If individuals are uncomfortable with visibility or resistant to direct feedback, they will follow the rules superficially but not internalize them. Over time, this creates a gap between process compliance and actual discipline. Culture does not follow systems; systems must align with culture, or deliberately reshape it over time.

6. **Financial Readiness:** Financial discipline is often misunderstood as cost control. In reality, it involves **intentional trade-offs**, including accepting short-term inefficiencies or increased costs to build long-term consistency.

Area	Measure	Acceptable Range	Risk Indicator
Error Tolerance	% of revenue	Moderate allowance	Too low = fear culture
Speed Value	Cost vs benefit	Positive impact	Negative = misalignment
Talent Investment	Incremental cost	Balanced	Excessive = unsustainable
System Value	Outcome vs cost	Clear advantage	Low return = overengineering
Customer Impact	Value improvement	Meaningful gain	Minimal change = misfit

For example, allowing a controlled level of error encourages decision-making and learning. Eliminating all errors creates fear, slows decisions, and reduces initiative. Similarly, investing in ownership-oriented talent may increase costs but significantly improve decision quality. Discipline is not about minimizing cost; it is about optimizing outcomes.

Beyond frameworks and tables, there are deeper questions that test intent.

For financial leadership, the challenge lies in prioritizing long-term discipline over short-term performance metrics. This requires accepting temporary declines in efficiency or profitability as the organization transitions.

For founders, the challenge is often control. Discipline requires distributing authority, allowing others to make decisions, and accepting that outcomes may not always align with personal expectations.

The Ultimate Alignment Questions

Before implementing any major change, leadership must confront the underlying intent.

For Financial Leadership:

- Can we prioritize long-term discipline over short-term outcomes?
- Are we willing to measure success beyond immediate metrics?
- Can we operate with full transparency of performance?

For Founders:

- Can control be distributed without constant intervention?
- Can better decisions come from others?
- Can uncertainty be accepted without reverting to control?

For Both:

- Are we optimizing for sustainability, not immediacy?
- Is our actual risk tolerance aligned with our stated one?
- Are we prepared for transparency and discomfort?

These questions connect directly to the chapter's central thesis: **discipline is a leadership choice before it is a system design.**

Together, leadership must align on a shared objective: building a system that outlasts individual control.

Decision Framework: Choosing the Right Path Forward

Once readiness is assessed, the organization must decide how to proceed.

Readiness Level	Recommendation	Next Step
High readiness	Full implementation	Commit and execute consistently
Moderate readiness	Controlled rollout	Start with a defined scope
Low readiness	Cultural preparation	Focus on visibility and ownership
Very low readiness	Delay implementation	Build leadership alignment first

The key here is alignment between ambition and readiness. Attempting full implementation without readiness leads to failure, not because the rules are wrong, but because the organization is not prepared to sustain them.

At this stage, the conversation shifts from organizational readiness to personal commitment. Frameworks, scorecards, and phased approaches can guide implementation, but they cannot substitute for leadership conviction. The organization will ultimately mirror the consistency or inconsistency of its leaders.

This is where many transformations quietly fail: not due to flawed design, but due to hesitation at the moment of enforcement. Before moving forward, leaders must step beyond analysis and confront a more direct question: *are we willing to live by the discipline we are about to demand?*

The Discipline Test

Before moving forward, leaders must confront a final, simple test:

- Will I follow every rule without exception?
- Will I remain consistent under pressure?
- Will I reinforce behavior instead of bypassing it?
- Am I prepared for discomfort and resistance?
- Will I prioritize long-term discipline over short-term ease?

If the answer to any of these is uncertain, the organization is not failing; it is simply not ready.

Before implementing any system or rule, organizations must recognize a fundamental truth: financial discipline cannot be installed; it must be chosen first. It begins with a conscious decision to operate consistently, accountably, and transparently, even when it is inconvenient. Without that choice, any structure introduced will remain superficial.

Once chosen, discipline has to be reinforced through everyday behavior. Leaders must follow the same rules they expect others to follow, decisions must reflect defined standards, and exceptions must remain rare and visible. Without consistent reinforcement, rules quickly become flexible, and systems lose their authority.

Sustaining discipline is what ultimately determines success. It requires applying the same standards over time, especially under pressure. The moment discipline becomes situational; it ceases to be discipline and becomes a preference.

This is where systems and rules play their role.

Systems can scale financial discipline, but only after it exists. Rules can enforce financial discipline, but only when they are consistently applied.

What makes financial discipline real is readiness, the willingness of the organization to live by what it defines. Without readiness, tools and rules remain structured but have no impact. With it, even the simplest systems become effective.

Practices That Create Immediate Discipline

One of the most consistent patterns across Financial Discipline Organizations is this: they do not wait for perfect systems to begin enforcing discipline.

Instead, they start with simple, visible practices that immediately shape behavior. These practices require no technology investment, no complex implementation, and no structural overhaul. What they require is consistency.

The goal is not sophistication. The goal is to create awareness, introduce friction, and reinforce accountability using the simplest possible mechanisms.

1. Immediate Visibility: A daily cash update forces the organization to stay grounded in reality. When financial position is visible every day, decisions naturally become more cautious and deliberate. This aligns directly with earlier principles: what is visible gets managed.

Practice	What to Do	Why It Works
Daily Cash Email	Share cash position, burn, and runway every morning	Visibility creates accountability

2. Pause Before Spending: This introduces deliberate friction into the system. Discipline-supporting systems are designed not just for efficiency, but for better decision-making. A simple pause often eliminates unnecessary spending without requiring any additional control mechanism.

Practice	What to Do	Why It Works
24-Hour Purchase Pause	Delay all spending above a fixed threshold	Slows impulsive decisions

3. Make Spending Public: When spending is visible across the organization, accountability shifts from hierarchical to social. This reinforces a key idea from earlier sections: peer pressure is often more effective than formal control.

Practice	What to Do	Why It Works
Public Spending Sheet	List all purchases above a threshold, visible to all	Peer visibility drives discipline

4. Cultural Shift: This practice moves the conversation from justification to reflection. Instead of hiding poor decisions, it normalizes learning from them, reinforcing the idea that discipline is built through **awareness and correction**, not avoidance.

Practice	What to Do	Why It Works
Weekly Question	Ask: "What did we spend on that didn't work?"	Encourages learning and ownership

5. Remove Before Adding: Complexity accumulates silently. This practice ensures that organizations actively remove unnecessary costs rather than continuously adding new ones.

Practice	What to Do	Why It Works
"Kill One Thing" Ritual	Eliminate one expense or subscription	Prevents cost accumulation

These practices succeed because they directly apply the principles established throughout this chapter:

- Visibility creates accountability
- Friction improves decisions

- Consistency builds discipline

They do not rely on systems. They rely on behavior.

Start Now: These are not initiatives to plan. They are actions to begin.

Cost	Time to Start	Expected Impact
Minimal	Immediate	Noticeable reduction in unnecessary spending

The most important step is the first one. Start today.

Stories of Discipline in Action

Financial Discipline Organizations are not defined by their tools; they are defined by how behavior changes when **visibility, accountability, and ownership** are introduced. The following stories are not about sophisticated systems. They are about simple rules, reinforced consistently, that transformed outcomes in measurable ways.

Turnaround Example of Discipline in Action

This example demonstrates a core principle of Financial Discipline Organizations: when financial reality is made visible, behavior changes faster than any system can enforce.

Metric	Before	After (Year 1)
Revenue	₹120 Cr	₹185 Cr
Profit/Loss	-₹8 Cr	+₹19 Cr
Cash	Critical	₹12 Cr
Receivables	45 days	21 days

The organization began with a familiar response to crisis: more controls, more approvals, more reports. The result was that the losses doubled.

The shift came not from tightening systems, but from changing behavior through transparency.

- On **Day 1**, every key employee could see the company's bank balance. The shock was immediate. Reality replaced assumptions. Within days, financial information moved from reports to conversations.
- By **Day 7**, profitability was made personal. Each unit, down to the operational level, could see its daily performance. This did not require a complex system. It required making the impact visible.
- Within **30 days**, a frontline observation uncovered inefficiency in operating behavior. A small change driven by awareness, not instruction, scaled across operations, generating meaningful savings. No audit, no consultant, no system upgrade, just visibility leading to action.
- By **Day 60**, customer behavior was also made visible. Payment delays were no longer hidden in reports; they were displayed openly. Accountability shifted from finance to the entire organization.
- By **Day 90**, improvements were no longer top-down. Individuals began identifying inefficiencies and acting on them directly. What emerged was not compliance but ownership.

Stage	Outcome
Initial error	Financial loss
Public sharing	Organizational awareness
System correction	Error reduction
Long-term impact	Significant savings

In traditional environments, mistakes are hidden. In disciplined organizations, they are surfaced.

A procurement error created a financial loss. Instead of concealment, the mistake was openly discussed. The focus was not on blame, but on understanding the cause. That single act triggered a cascade of similar acts, near-miss patterns emerged, and corrective mechanisms were introduced.

Within months, error rates declined significantly. The financial benefit far exceeded the original loss. Discipline is not built by preventing mistakes; it is built by learning from them quickly and visibly.

The Power of Inclusion

Role	Observation	Impact
Frontline employee	Identified inefficiency	Cost savings
Organization	Acted on insight	Sustained improvement

When financial information is shared broadly, ownership expands beyond roles and titles. Individuals who are closest to operations often have the clearest view of inefficiencies.

In this case, a simple observation enabled by access to information led to the identification of unnecessary costs. Authority was given to act, and results followed. The outcome was not just cost reduction, but a reinforcement of a core principle: **everyone is responsible for financial outcomes.**

Across these examples, a consistent pattern emerges. The improvements did not come from introducing more sophisticated systems or tighter controls, but from making financial reality visible and actionable. When numbers were no longer confined to reports and instead became part of daily conversations, behavior shifted. Individuals at all levels began to understand their impact, question inefficiencies, and take ownership of outcomes.

What started as isolated actions quickly compounded into broader cultural change. These stories reinforce a central idea of Financial Discipline Organizations: when discipline is made visible and personal, it scales naturally without complex tools.

Traditional Thinking	Discipline Reality	Outcome
Control creates discipline	Visibility creates discipline	Faster behavior change
Systems drive outcomes	Behavior drives outcomes	Sustainable improvement
Information should be restricted.	Information should be shared	Higher ownership
Decisions belong to leadership.	Insight exists across levels	Better solutions

Systems do not create financial discipline; it is sustained by behavior. Tools can accelerate, enforce, and scale, but they cannot replace ownership, judgment, or accountability. When organizations rely on systems without first establishing discipline, they create visibility without action and control without impact.

The path is clear: behavior comes first. Organizations that succeed make financial reality visible, introduce thoughtful friction, and ensure accountability is personal. Systems then follow, not as solutions, but as amplifiers of consistent behavior.

At its core, financial discipline is a choice to prioritize consistency over convenience and long-term outcomes over short-term ease. That choice is tested under pressure, when exceptions are tempting, and speed competes with judgment. In the end, the question is simple: will discipline hold when systems don't?

Because when discipline is real, systems strengthen it. When it isn't, the system only exposes it.

9

INSTITUTIONALIZING ACCOUNTABILITY

There's an employee in front of you. Their hands are behind their back, necks bowed almost guiltily. There's a report on your desk—a simple explanation of the financial blunder discovered and how it will be resolved. As you read the paper, you can see the employee shrink even more.

As if it's their worst day ever.

They stand there, almost like a chastised child. But there's something that makes you hold back your reprimands. Despite the size of the blunder and its consequences, your employees have started to come forward even when they make mistakes. They've begun to value communication and solving the issue rather than avoiding taking responsibility. They're actively keeping themselves accountable for all their decisions. Accountability is, without a doubt, a cornerstone of sustained financial discipline, effectively transforming it from a temporary initiative into a permanent organizational capability. Accountability keeps financial systems and strategies from crumbling, helping them remain strong and resilient through everyday operations and projects.

Accountability of It All

Accountability is the state of being required to justify and substantiate your actions. Financial accountability is necessary to ensure that money is used and managed responsibly. This accountability only works when every member of the company participates in maintaining it. People need to use company money wisely, follow the outlined rules, and be *honest* about how they manage their own money. Accountability and responsibility go hand in hand, meant to ensure the company builds trust, makes smart financial decisions, and keeps everyone on track for long-term success. Financial accountability pushes transparency, diligence, compliance, risk management, and performance measurement.

Why is accountability so integral to financial discipline?

Being the foundation of financial success, accountability allows:

1. Cultivates ownership at every level
2. Transforms abstract goals into concrete actions
3. Prevents "Not My Job" Syndrome
4. Creates Sustainable Behavior Change
5. Enables early warning systems

Accountability allows a cascading effect, with individual accountability positively affecting team performance, eliciting agreeable and exemplary department results, and ultimately leading to organizational success. HDFC Bank, one of India's most famous, popular, and trusted banks, didn't start popular. Instead, they started as a relatively new private bank in 1994, with ₹100 crore capital, zero customers, and competing against government banks. So how did they grow to the position they hold today?

Adita Puri had three vital rules:

1. Every branch was to have a profit center with published Profits and Losses.

2. Every loan was to be treated like the employee's baby; the relationship manager would own it till it was repaid.
3. Every employee was to conduct themselves and treat themselves as the owner, allotted ESOPs.

They also employed key mechanisms to keep employees motivated and maintain financial discipline.

- **Traffic light system:** where green represents targets that are hit and gives the employees full bonuses; yellow is a warning for not hitting all targets, giving employees half bonuses; red signifies a failure in meeting targets and gives employees no bonuses or PIP.
- **Daily 8:30 am meeting:** In each meeting, ten leaders get two minutes each to go over yesterday's numbers and today's plan. A purely action-focused discussion where every leader brings solutions with no excuses.
- **Ownership policy:** Branch managers and departments own loan portfolios, which allows them to maintain 0.3% NPA against the industry's 5%.

The Results

Metric	Start (1994)	End (2025)	Growth
Branches	1	9400	9,400x
Revenue	₹100 cr	₹3.0 lakh cr	1,500x
Market Cap	₹300 cr	₹15 lakh cr	2,600x
NPAs	-	<1.5%	Best in India

So why did things work out so splendidly for HDFC Bank in places where others might have crumbled or collapsed?

There were clear indications on multiple occasions about what they were aspiring to meet, with giving everyone equity, due to the "owners never let businesses fail" mindset. They never hid behind obscure committees; instead, they put names to every single action. Problems were caught early, ensuring accountability almost every day.

And finally, metrics were made public, enforcing peer pressure for people to perform better.

All-Encompassing Financial Discipline

The importance of **cross-functional clarity**:

Finance vs operations vs marketing: Who owns what? Who signs off on what?

RACI matrix for financial decision points

Now, it can seem logical to focus only on finances, given that financial discipline is the word. However, let me be the first to say that financial discipline can be applied in many more places—and not doing so could lead to unexpected setbacks.

Each part of the organization has its own aspects and contributions to financial discipline.

The finance team acts as the translator, the predictor, the clarifier, and the trainer. They convert potential plans and strategies into simpler language and help employees understand exactly how finances can move forward with the proposals. They offer candid ideas about how it would play out and what the outcomes and future may look like if they go forward with the plan.

They ensure the company is aware of predictions and possibilities, always keeping an eye on how finances may be sinking and which precautionary measures the company would benefit from. The finance team is also meant to speed up processes by establishing clarity and removing confusion, so that other departments can continue their tasks without much delay.

They make their processes, knowledge, and know-how more accessible and digestible to other department members, so that any non-trained employee can pick them up just as easily. This makes it easier to expedite the process and for people to explain it to others without confusion. Next, leaders are meant to present themselves as the model for financial discipline. They have to display the kind of conduct employees are to follow and understand the expectations set for them. All of their good financial decisions act as a manual for other employees, offering a domino effect of good financial choices.

They're meant to set the tone by making financial discipline of the utmost importance. By novelizing and incentivizing the process, they get employees on board with the mindset. A rewards approach helps teams feel more motivated to work hard at embodying the mindset. This is another reason leaders will always ensure the process is an exchange rather than a demand. Plus, leaders show clear processes for prioritizing honesty, delivering value, aligning authority with accountability, and conducting failed experiments with sound financial rationale to back them. Project managers in the same strain have to ensure that their stack- up of cases benefits the company. Every project needs an ROI model; returns must be tracked regularly, whether actual or projected. Any project that deviates from expectations or the outlined format must be removed promptly.

They should be conservative and shrewd with finances, firm about balancing overspending with budget cuts, and ensure burn rates are visible to stakeholders. It's project managers who are meant to escalate when financial plans are jeopardized, but also celebrate when teams successfully remain under budget. Additionally, it's project managers who must track actual ROI, course-correct when value isn't being delivered as required, and document processes that have delivered positive results for future projects. The Board and Audit Committee is another team with multiple responsibilities that require them to step up.

It's their responsibility to set strategic financial boundaries, establish ROI thresholds for projects, define risk tolerance frameworks, manage capital allocation, and provide guidance on clearing the burn rate.

It's always the board that has to ask questions others would rather not ask, including any misses, failures, possibilities for growth, and the harsher realities of the company. They are also the main group to be concerned with sustainability and growth, to manage both overspending and underspending, to boost financial discipline, and to safeguard investments. Most of all, it's the board and audit committee that have to hold leadership accountable, regularly reviewing the pace of decision-making, conducting surveys on empowerment, and establishing benchmark metrics of efficiency.

The Accountability matrix

Decision Type	Finance	CxO	BU Head	PM	Board
Strategic Capital Allocation	Analyze	Recommend	Input	-	Approve
Unit Budget Setting	Guide	Approve	Own	-	Review
Project ROI	Validate	Review	Approve	Own	-
Vendor Negotiations	Support	-	Approve	Execute	-
Kill Decisions	Flag	Approve	Recommend	Execute	Review
Process Optimization	Enable	Champion	Drive	Execute	-

Let's analyze Jet Airways' collapse to see how a failure to take accountability can further complicate and deteriorate the company's condition, especially when already stressed.

In 2018-19, India's premier airline was going through a visible downward spiral. They were in more than ₹8,000 crore in debt, salaries had been unpaid for months, planes were being grounded daily, and nobody knew who was in charge or to whom they were reporting.

So why is such an accountability void suddenly finding itself forming here?

It's essentially a game of "Who's Actually Running the Company?" where we have:

Founder: "I'm Chairman."

Lenders: "We control the board."

Etihad (Partner): "We have veto rights."

CEO: "I need approvals for everything."

CFO: "I can't access cash without three signatures."

COO: "I can't ground unsafe planes without board approval."

And the result that we're left with is a complete paralysis of all tasks and movement.

The Role Confusion Matrix

Decision	Who Thought They Owned It	Who Actually Decided	Result
Route planning	CEO	Founder	Loss-making routes continued
Crew scheduling	Operations	HR	Pilots walked out
Vendor payments	CFO	Treasury	Fuel supply stopped
Safety decisions	Engineering	Finance	Planes flew unsafe
Pricing	Revenue team	Goyal's secretary	Irrational pricing

There are five fatal accountability gaps that Jet Airways created through its actions, all of which contributed to its gradual collapse.

- **Aircraft lease payments:** week 1: CFO States, "treasury handles this"; treasury says, "need board approval"; board demands, "need lender consent"; lenders reply, "need business plan first". By week 8, lessors repossess planes.
- **Fuel payments:** in the morning, the fuel company threatens to cut supplies; at noon, five executives meet but make no decision; in the evening, flights are canceled, leaving passengers stranded. The next day, the same meeting occurs with no resolution.
- **Salary crisis:** HR insists, "finance must release funds"; finance responds, "need CEO approval"; the CEO states, "need board clearance"; the board adds, "need lender permission"; lenders request, "show us a turnaround plan". Consequently, engineers and pilots quit en masse.
- **Safety decisions:** an engineer states, "this plane needs grounding"; the ops head says, "check with commercial"; commercial says, "we need the capacity"; safety head remarks, "not my call anymore"; the plane flies anyway.
- **Customer refunds:** customer service says, "finance must approve"; finance claims, "no cash available"; Treasury insists, "Need CEO sign-off"; the CEO says, "Board must decide". An unresolved ₹1,800 crore in booking refunds remains outstanding.

The Death Spiral

Month 1: Role confusion → Delayed decisions

Month 3: Delayed decisions → Vendor exits

Month 6: Vendor exits → Operations collapse

Month 9: Total shutdown

Jet Airways is a perfect example to represent how certain financial "decisions" are actually holes in discipline, no matter how much a boss wants to think otherwise. Instead, the company is faced with harsh truths, i.e.:

1. Multiple bosses = No boss
2. Shared accountability = No accountability
3. Consensus requirement = Decision paralysis
4. Veto without ownership = Guaranteed failure

Creating FD Champions

Whenever new rules and policies are introduced to be followed, systems always require enforcers. Well, your FD champions are exactly that—smart and able enforcers who can ensure that financial discipline sinks into work seamlessly. It's a firewall against malware that could compromise your organization's internal systems.

They're the ops manager who spots a $100K saving in shipping routes, the engineer who realizes cloud costs can drop 40% with simple scheduling, the marketer who kills a million-dollar campaign that isn't converting. They live in the business, speak the language of their function, but think like owners.

FD Champions are meant to be people who get the job done, not convenient-to-have employees who excel and make things look organized (though those are required skills as well). They solve problems like it's no one's business. They have a better idea of how operations are supposed to progress than anyone else, and have credibility because they've shipped product, closed deals, or fixed operations. When they talk financial sense, teams listen because they've earned respect through operational excellence, not financial theory.

FD Champions are:

1. Sensitive to inefficiency. Their top priority is ensuring that none of the tasks undertaken are completed inefficiently. They make sure no unnecessary license expenditure is incurred, spot duplicate vendors, zombie subscriptions, and actions or processes that burn money without justification.
2. If there's anyone good at communicating the needs of finance teams to general teams who have no idea about finance, it's the FD champions. They're experts at twisting conversations to ensure that, eventually, the end goal is met, and the people get what they wanted.
3. FD champions are dead set on getting what they want. If they know that value's going to pour out of a deal, they're set on working out everything required for it. They know the exact questions to ask that their peers might be too awkward or reluctant to ask—the questions that get the company the value it wants.

However, FD Champions are **not**:

1. **Mini-CFOs:** CFOs have a completely different job, with approving and rejecting, making sure finances don't dip, and overseeing all the deals made. But FD Champions are there to figure out the processes that work. They want to get those values in the company's balance sheets, and they pull out all stops to make sure it happens.
2. **Budget Managers:** FD Champions aren't there to see whether people are sticking to the budget and wave them away from accidentally overspending. They're there to boost value, and if that means blowing a budget out of the water to get 10x the return, they'll happily press the spend button without a second thought.

These Financial Discipline Champions are not meant to be another layer in the hierarchy that monitors or manages finances; they exist to further and develop value with deals that benefit the company. They are the spearheads in financial discipline, being viewed as a business function.

So, how do you find and pin down these champions? It's simple. You follow the Anti-Recruiting Process.

In contrast to recruiting, FD champions exist within the company—you have to sniff them out. There are always behavioral tips that let you know when you've found your champion. They're not exactly subtle in their pursuits to boost value in their line of tasks. Once you find them, it's just about turning their abilities to the entire organization.

1. **The Questioners:** Nothing is saved from being questioned. Every point in a presentation, line in a report, and comment in an update needs to be substantiated. These champions can't handle every aspect of the plan not being hashed out with zero corners cut. Every aspect that others might not have even thought to question is pulled out viciously by them.
2. **The Connectors:** Impeccable at reading into possible downturns in plans, future issues, deals that look sweet but sour over time, and seamless trade-offs. These champions are especially skilled at stepping back and looking at the whole picture, successfully connecting the teams and numbers in each deal.
3. **The Fixers:** Like handypersons, they patch up any loose threads and possible holes in any plan. They work on things without anyone pointing out errors, as if an error sensor rests in their head.

Red Flags to Avoid

1. The Penny Pincher: Saves cents while missing dollars
2. The Policy Wonk: Loves rules more than results
3. The Empire Builder: Wants the title, not the impact
4. The Finance Wannabe: Should join finance instead

You know your Financial Discipline Champions are successfully calibrated when:

1. Department heads brag about their champion's saves
2. Finance asks champions for input on policies
3. Vendors fear negotiating with your company
4. New hires are told, "Talk to the champion before buying anything."
5. Other companies try to poach your champions

The aim isn't to develop mini-CFOs or corporate enforcers. It's to integrate the owners' mindset throughout the organization. When employees view company spending as personal, see value as their own equity, and consider waste as an enemy, you do more than just cut costs—you foster a cultural shift. Ultimately, culture, rather than controls, drives enduring financial discipline.

The Consequences of Any Action

There will be times when you can tell a person isn't taking their job seriously, but it's not a mistake you can afford to let slide when it interferes with the financial discipline of the company. While mistakes are inevitable during the learning curve, companies have a limited number of attempts they can accept.

Instead, the best approach to take to curb these mistakes, or at least deal with them appropriately, would be to set up an escalation system. The system would have three tiers, in increasing order of offense.

1. The yellow flags, for minor or first offenses. These would be warnings for passing the budget by 10%, missing any ROI targets, or even failing to negotiate with a vendor properly. Small offenses can become less frequent with time and increased skill. They can be remedied easily. A proper response in such a case would be to have the person receive coaching within 24 hours, undergo a root-cause analysis, and remediate the issue. It would then be finished with a team discussion so everyone can understand the mistake made, how to avoid it, and why it is paramount that they rise above it.
2. Orange flags would represent repeat mistakes or a pattern of mistakes. Categorized under this section would be mistakes such as repeatedly missing the budget, consistent ROI failures, and a breakdown in team financial discipline. The proper response in such a situation is to review within 48 hours, implement a 30-day improvement plan, and finally oversee their financial decisions for a while.
3. Finally, red flags would represent material and willful financial blunders. These would include hidden losses or financial or account manipulation, unauthorized major spending, and deliberate circumvention of rules. Due to the nature of the decisions and the sheer gravity of the situation, there would be a CEO/CFO review on the same day, a spending freeze, and a potential termination. This isn't about shame - it's about protecting the organization and sending a clear message that financial discipline isn't optional.

As usual, the approach that works wonders here is a three-tier/three-strike system that allows employees to visualize actual progress and consequences while imbuing financial discipline into company operations.

The first strike would result in weekly CFO reviews, mandatory offset finding before any spending, a 10% budget reduction, and mandatory financial training.

The second strike would be an escalation, with a 20% budget cut, a hiring freeze, frozen bonuses, and a compulsory finance co-signature requirement on all proposals.

The third and final strike would involve the permanent removal of budget authority, either demotion or termination of the employee, followed by a public session to educate the rest of the organization.

The only way people will stop any negative behavior that ruins financial discipline is by making remedial action either terrifying or unbearable, so they decide on their own to stop. By implementing actions such as requiring a 10-page business case, a 72-hour cooling period, full leadership team presentations, and even docking 10% of bonuses for each excuse request, your employees will gradually learn that lackadaisical financial discipline is painful, and they're not ready to deal with it.

You must kill common excuses immediately, track every exception publicly, and make the cost visible to peers.

The main point you're trying to drive with these harsh measures is that the pattern that has slowly developed needs to die, for everyone's benefit. Otherwise, changes would need to be made to roles—a change that no one would really appreciate. The organization needs to understand that it is this prudence and care that define accountability. The team needs to understand that the leader's choices affect everyone on the team and, in turn, like a spider's web, the rest of the company. These feelings need to be ingrained in everyone's work attitude until everyone understands that budgets are commitments, not suggestions; that exceptions are unacceptable; and that repeated disregard of orders is punishable.

The ultimate test is simple: would this person manage their own money this way? If they wouldn't, then it becomes clear that the issue is not skill, but instead their values and how they view the company's finances. Each issue that remains unaddressed or overlooked sends the message that discipline is optional. Instead, you have to stay alert, respond quickly, transparently, and thoughtfully.

Remember, the goal is not just changing one person's habits. It's strengthening the organization's culture of financial discipline.

Transparency is vital for financial discipline, especially when you always need a crystal-clear view of how the financial internals are looking. It's this transparency that also jumpstarts accountability among employees. No one wants to be the only one not keeping up with financial discipline, becoming the stain on the otherwise perfect record. They don't want to underperform and have everyone see it, nor do they want their team to be beaten by another's metrics. And when there's transparency, people can understand cognitively why the decision is a good one and hence be more on board with supporting it.

So what might you want to present to employees and stakeholders more?

You can start with:

1. Burn rate by team
2. Budget vs. actual
3. ROI by project
4. Efficiency scores
5. Waste identified

The 3-Second Rule: Anyone should understand performance in 3 seconds - green (good), yellow (warning), red (failing).

Additionally, it would help more if you made efforts to share news, even if it's bad, quickly with the team.

By sharing information without a second thought, the receiving parties feel like they can trust you to keep them updated in any situation. So you share:

1. Bad news within 24 hours
2. Context with every number
3. Names on every metric
4. Solutions for every problem

When CEOs share their failures publicly, hiding becomes culturally impossible. You can also encourage accountability among peers by intentionally providing platforms and spaces for them to share or divulge information. This would cultivate honesty and accountability as habits, making it second nature to be direct and transparent about the situation.

For example, you can start hosting "Weekly Finance Fridays" where teams present their financial performance to each other rather than to management. This can help them prepare for presenting to management, facilitate brainstorming between teams on how to resolve issues or improve budgeting, and foster a more harmonious relationship between teams.

You can establish efficient league tables that instill a competitive spirit among employees and bring a lighthearted competitive spirit into relationships. You can also declare "waste bounties" where people are praised and given rewards for finding inaccuracies and inefficiencies. This ensures that:

1. Bad news travels up fast
2. Teams demand more data
3. Voluntary sharing increases
4. Hiding feels wrong

The People Layer is the key to accountability within the FDO framework.

While Process provides standardization and Price focuses on optimization, it is People who carry out the work, make decisions, and ultimately decide whether financial discipline is implemented or remains just theory.

Without Accountability,

1. People → Make decisions in silos
2. Process → Gets bypassed when inconvenient
3. Price → Becomes "someone else's problem." With Accountability:
4. People → Own financial outcomes personally
5. Process → Becomes a non-negotiable discipline
6. Price → Reflects collective commitment

The people-accountability matrix

People Element	Without Accountability	With Accountability
Individual Contributors	"Not my budget."	"I impact every dollar."
Managers	Report numbers	Own variances
Leaders	Set targets	Model discipline
Teams	Work in isolation	Share P&L ownership
Culture	Blame & hide	Learn & improve

10

WHAT FOUNDERS, BOARDS & CXOS MUST KNOW

"Walk the walk to talk the talk."

The most important part of implementing financial discipline is knowing that employees are internalizing it by watching the top layer of the company hierarchy. If Leaders and founders follow the ideal behavior marked out for financial discipline, employees fall in line easily and mimic their superiors. However, the moment they realize that their leaders aren't taking that "discipline" seriously, their own motivation crumbles and the discipline shatters.

Financial discipline has never been an issue for the finance team. Financial discipline begins at the top. Founders, boards, and CXOs must set the tone, oversee governance, and stay actively involved in the making, monitoring, and enforcement of financial decisions. Trust begins with financial clarity.

Leadership Domino Effect

The management can create the outline of financial discipline and pen down rules that people refer to, but the actual act of following has to happen through leaders deciding what they want to represent.

Leaders are meant to demonstrate what they really care about through decisions that promote financial discipline. Whether they'll sacrifice short-term gains for long-term financial health, ensuring people know their priorities.

It's also because leaders decide how to allocate resources, energy, or attention to which projects. Leaders control the flow of time, talent, and capital, which means they decide which initiatives get funded or rejected, which metrics appear on dashboards, and which behaviors are praised or penalized.

Things that leaders accept or tolerate are seen as encouraged. Thus, if no attention is paid to missed budgets, "creative" accounting, lavish spending, and short-term thinking, employees gradually learn that these behaviors will go unpunished. All semblance of financial discipline in the company crumbles. A leader may think it's a small choice in their decision, but it's the domino effect of one careless decision. The CEO who spends extravagantly on private jets gives the impression that wasteful spending on business trips will be overlooked. A leader who takes lower pay cuts during times of strife sends a very different message from one who continues to take large cuts regardless of the company's state.

Finance teams can provide the company with analyses, frameworks, and guardrails, but they cannot help with the hierarchical and bureaucratic challenges that may arise. Financial discipline is upheld by the decisions made by those who uphold it. At the end of the day, the most significant responsibility for upholding it lies with those who have the most decision-making power, hence the leaders.

The leaders have the authority, visibility, and influence to ensure their choices reflect disciplined thinking. Finance might be able to keep score, but leadership is what determines how the game is played.

Blind Spots

Founders of companies, without a doubt, bring passion, innovation, and drive to the table, but there's also a clear lack of attention to preventing some predictable financial discipline failures. For example: treating money carelessly. Between being assured that everything will be solved once growth and revenue hit the company, seeing company financial resources as personal reserves, and treating them carelessly, leaders forget that prudence with finances is vital for maintaining discipline.

Another example is prioritizing speed over building reliable structures. They put structures on the back burner, assuming that they can get to them once the company has reached greater heights, but when you look back at your company at that point, all you will see is a plethora of accumulated bad habits.

Rather than focusing on rectifying bad habits later on, focus on building good habits and foundations now. This can also be seen with companies that reward "saves" and "heroes" in projects rather than prevention and consistency. There are also obvious mistakes in what companies tend to prioritize along the journey, such as user growth over retention or PR wins over unit economics.

Successful founders are those who have a vision enabled by financial discipline, set the right culture early on, and fulfill all expectations from Year 1 through Year 5. Founders who maintain financial discipline from Day 1 have more freedom to pursue their vision, not less—the constraints they accept early become the foundation for sustainable growth later.

Founders should focus on the company's survival and sustainable growth, not reckless growth at any cost.

Of all details they should be paying attention to, the most important are:

1. **Money:** Leaders should monitor cash balances, burn rates, and runway monthly. The question "when do we run out of money?" should always have an answer.
2. **Unit Economics:** Things like CAC payback, gross margins, and LTV always need to be tracked. There should always be a path to profitability for every single customer.
3. **Performance vs Plan:** Monthly analyses should be reviewed monthly, where each analysis also offers explanations for any variances above 20%.
4. **Risk:** Every quarter, there should be a risk register and stress test, which helps leaders study what may damage or kill the company. Additionally, migration plans should be in place and ready to be implemented at any time.
5. **Capital Allocation:** All major investments need to be approved first, and all ROI and payback periods must be questioned before approval. Additionally, value creation or destruction should be tracked.

Finally, three absolute requirements that leaders should be attending to are:

1. Independent Audit Committee with financial expertise
2. Direct Access to the CFO and auditors without the CEO
3. Pre-defined Consequences for missing targets

The most important part of this process is ensuring the board doesn't slack on questioning its employees and the finance department. There are crucial aspects and topics that the board cannot decline to question; otherwise, the financial discipline or process may fall apart.

These questions include:

1. Survival questions like "what is our exact cash balance burn rate?" "When do we hit cash zero?", and "Are we default dead or default alive?"
2. Economics questions like "walk me through the unit economics", "what percentage of customers are profitable", and "if we stopped growing, would we eventually become profitable?"
3. Performance questions like "Show me the revenue per employee for the last 6 quarters", "What are our top 3 areas of wasted spend?", and "Which investments from last year failed to deliver ROI?"
4. Risk Assessment Questions like "What are three things that could kill this company?" "What happens if revenue drops tomorrow?", and "Where are we most in danger of a single failure?"
5. Strategy Alignment Questions like "Does our spending match our priorities?", "What unnecessary costs are we maintaining out of habit?" or "Are we investing in growth or just maintaining positions?"
6. Culture Questions like "Does every executive understand unit economics?" or "Does every employee understand our burn rates?"

And eventually, you understand that you are asking the right questions, like when your management is prepared with answers because they know you'll enquire on certain topics. Or when you see that the presentations have started including downside scenarios to every proposal, indicating that they've started looking into ideas with a multi- dimensional view rather than just the benefits.

Or even when negative outcomes or bad news make their way to you fast, rather than right before a deadline. Seeing changes in your team's work, like simpler metrics dashboards and trade-offs being debated openly, is a staggering review of how well your efforts are being received.

Trust the Foundation

Trust is a cornerstone of handling money and greatly impacts the relations you have with many teams.

1. **Investors:** The line between investors viewing spending as reckless cash burning or spending for a sustainable growth plan is thin, and without trust, can be transformed into something unsightly. Companies should maintain trust by consistently hitting their goals at 2 to 3x the valuations and closing rounds 50% faster. When you share your metrics with others, investors become convenient references and testaments to your responsible money habits.
2. **Lenders:** Startups are categorized from high risk to professionally managed by banks, based on cash flows and forecasts. Strong financial discipline results in Prime + 2-4% rates compared to 8-12%, doubles available credit, and removes the need for personal guarantees. The essential factors include keeping books audit-ready, updating 13-week cash flow forecasts weekly, and consistently meeting covenants.
3. **Team Morale:** When leadership shows financial discipline, employees stop fearing surprise layoffs and begin thinking like owners. Turnover falls below 10%, employer ratings improve, and 90% of staff feel confident about the company's future. Regular weekly updates on burn rate and runway, along with

recognizing efficiency achievements, shift the culture from "spend it or lose it" to "every dollar matters."

4. **Vendor Partnerships:** Disciplined companies secure Net 60 payment terms, enjoy 20-40% discounts, and gain strategic partnership opportunities because vendors recognize their long-term stability. Paying invoices within 15 days, sharing three-year growth plans, and holding quarterly business reviews shift vendor relationships from simple transactions to strategic alliances. As a result, many vendors become investors and offer exclusive features to financially disciplined partners.

Without discipline, you'll have constant dependence on emergency funding, extremely bad terms from financial institutions, low morale, which leads to talent exodus, resulting in poor execution, higher costs, and restarting the vicious cycle with more emergencies.

With discipline, however, you unearth efficient growth on premium terms, boosting morale and helping the company become a talent magnet, enabling excellent execution, lower costs, and greater efficiency. The difference quickly accumulates, leading to either a downward spiral or a lasting competitive edge within 12-18 months.

TVS Group's Financial Discipline

The story of the TVS Group is not defined by rapid expansion or headline growth. It is defined by a consistent preference for financial discipline as a strategic operating choice. Long before electrification, platform expansion, or logistics diversification became fashionable, TVS embedded cost consciousness and capital restraint into how it built businesses.

Across operating companies and investment arms, the common thread is not performance metrics, but decision quality. TVS demonstrates that financial discipline is not about slowing down—it is about ensuring that every step forward is sustainable. That discipline, practiced consistently, becomes a competitive advantage that compounds quietly over time.

Their ease and stability represented:

1. Learning from past investments
2. Adapting to changing market conditions
3. Maintaining return discipline

With a company like TVS that consistently shares its annual reports, it demonstrates its commitment to giving back to its communities through investments in training institutions and schools. Their view of finance is not about penny-pinching but passing resources forward, allowing long-term value creation, including social investments. It becomes increasingly obvious with their finances and business transactions that their see cost management approach is about ensuring every rupee enables maximum value-creation and invests in future technologies.

The Mindset Shift

What founders need to ensure that they adopt healthier mindsets—aspects that push financial discipline and help the company stand stronger.

Strategic Planning: Financial Discipline as North Star

Time and again, companies have learned that the traditional approach is no longer giving them what they need, and is definitely not helping them keep up with competitors. So what companies need to do is start treating financial discipline like the North Star, an unfailing beacon to follow every time things get confusing, holding confidence that it will lead them back home.

FINANCIAL DISCIPLINE ORGANIZATION

Define Success Metrics	Stress Test Every Strategy	Build Kill Switches
Not: "Be market Leader" But: Achieve 30% market share with 40% gross margins" Not: "International expansion" But: "3 profitable markets with <18 months payback"	What's the cash requirement? What's the payback period? What's the downside scenario? Where's the exit ramp?	Pre-define failure criteria Set investment limits Create stage points Mandate pivot points Example: New Product Launch **Phase 1:** $500k to MVP (Kill if < 100 customers) **Phase 2**: $1.5M for scale (Kill if CAC> $1000) **Phase 3:** $3M for growth (Kill if margin <30%)

Companies with traditional processes would start with a vision, go through the process while adding initiatives, calculate potential costs, find reliable funding, and "hope it works." But now we know this is not the most reliable way to achieve growth. Instead, companies are committing to a more disciplined approach.

They start with unit economics, figuring out the projectable sustainability, and then model a sustainable state. These companies work backward to their milestones, and don't spend money carelessly.

Instead, they fund purely the value-creating steps. And when they have all of this set up, they measure ROI relentlessly to ensure they never dip below their projected revenues and profits.

Strategic Planning Through a Financial Lens

Fundraising: Capital as a Strategic Weapon

Sometimes, companies never have a clear idea of how to handle or raise capital, leaving them in a precarious financial position.

So, to understand the kind of capital and funds that need to be raised, you and your team have to ask yourselves certain questions, like: "Do we need capital or discipline?" "What's the value creation per dollar?" "Can we bootstrap this milestone?" Then you have to estimate how much you might need to raise. In traditional methods, people seemed to default to simply "raising as much capital as possible." However, with a more disciplined financial approach, one should focus on raising capital for specific value creation.

A formula people have started following is

Capital Need = (Burn × Months to Milestone) + Buffer.

Buffer = 6 months (not 18-24)

Companies also need to choose investors by discipline alignment. Instead of grabbing "grow at all costs" investors, leaders should be eyeing "sustainable growth" investors. They need to be prepared to answer the question: "Tell me about a portfolio failure." And most of all, they should have a good grasp on post-mortem culture.

While traditional approaches often describe themselves as "raising $50M to capture market," new strategies specify goals like "raising $20M to validate unit economics at scale, then securing additional growth capital."

Capital Deployment

An investment committee is meant to oversee investment policies, the selection of advisors, investment strategies, and fund performance to achieve the best possible outcome for the beneficiaries. A well-functioning investment committee always outlines its responsibilities clearly. It involves people with diverse backgrounds and expertise to ensure it can bring together perspectives from differing viewpoints.

Some committees make the mistake of spending too much time on investment manager oversight and not enough on asset allocation discussions and reviews.

So your team should spend a good amount of their time ensuring investments and assets are being assigned to profitable and valuable endeavors. Investment committee mindsets are sharp and particular when handling funds; hence, adopting this mindset ensures that all endeavors the company heads pursue reap valuable benefits.

This also includes following a specific distribution when allocating funds. For example, the 70/20/10 rules where 70% of funds go into proven ROI activities, 20% into experiments and endeavors that seem promising, and the last 10% into long-shot bets, an amount of money you can afford to use on trial-and-error decisions. Finally, the team should prioritize a monthly capital review, where they examine each initiative and essentially initiate a culling. The top 3 are funded from previous years or quarters; the bottom four are cut from the list. This ensures the company isn't needlessly pouring money into initiatives that aren't serving them and are instead pulling down their profits and revenues. Not changing budget allocations for long periods can lead to oversight of endeavors that drain the company's assets.

Building Audit-Ready Financial Discipline: Quick Guide

Core Principles

1. **Document Everything:** No transaction without a paper trail
2. **Real-time Recording:** Same-day entries, no backlogs
3. **No Override:** Even founders follow the approval matrix
4. **Segregate Duties:** Approver ≠ Executor

The 3-Layer Framework

Systems

1. Cloud accounting software
2. Automated approval workflows

3. Bank feed integrations
4. Exception alerts

Structure

1. Clear approval hierarchies
2. Monthly internal audits
3. Vendor payment schedules
4. 5-day month-end close

Culture

1. Reward transparency
2. Punish cover-ups, not mistakes
3. Monthly financial training
4. Share audit results

Daily Essentials

1. Morning cash position
2. Expense pre-approvals
3. Bank reconciliation
4. Document filing

Red Flags to Watch

1. Delayed reporting
2. Frequent "adjustments."
3. Related party transactions
4. Finance team turnover
5. Vendor payment delays

Audit-Ready Checklist

1. Updated bank reconciliations
2. Filed supporting documents
3. Completed compliance certificates
4. Documented approvals
5. Current contracts repository

Quick Wins

1. Week 1: Implement expense approval app
2. Month 1: Complete first internal audit
3. Quarter 1: Automate bank reconciliation
4. Year 1: Achieve a clean audit report

Remember

1. Small compromises → Big frauds
2. Financial discipline = Stakeholder trust
3. Better to be audit-ready than audit-worried
4. Boring processes prevent exciting disasters

Start Now: Pick one process. Fix it today. Build momentum.

In financial discipline, shortcuts are just future scandals waiting to happen.

Financial discipline doesn't crumble overnight. There are always signs, no matter how subtle or obvious, which is why leaders always need to be cognizant and painfully aware of how they hold the key to making discipline a success.

From aspects as simple as their language and how they frame questions to more complex nuances like transparency and hiring specifications, leaders can subtly influence their employees to walk in the same shoes, thereby leading the company toward a more financially secure and disciplined conduct and by committing to acts like staying in modest hotels, choosing candidates with spectacular financial acumen and know-how, prioritizing a finance- forward mindset with accountability, and focusing on the most important financial aspects like ROI, unit economics of products, budgets, and allocation of resources.

Leaders also contribute appropriately when they commit to actions like rejecting bad-fit customers even if the quota hasn't been met, publishing prices publicly when possible, building value before raising prices, revealing ROIs openly, over-delivering consistently to maintain trust, sharing customer success metrics publicly, monitoring success proactively, and optimizing for lifetime value, not just current value.

Though each action seems small on its own, when combined, leaders successfully create an iron wall of financial discipline that will remain rooted within the company's actions for a long time.

11

STAKEHOLDERS – LENDERS, INVESTORS & REGULATORS

I have sat in on enough lender-borrower meetings as a banker to recognize the pattern. The slides are polished. The projections climb sharply upward. The founder speaks with confidence, momentum, and conviction. Revenue is doubling. Market opportunity is massive. The story is compelling.

Then something unexpected happens.

A senior investor or lender sits back, rather than leaning forward. There are no questions about market size or valuation; rather, the pause continues. At last, out of the quiet, a question breaks the energy in the room: "How do you really control this growth?" The founder's response includes numbers, systems, and assurances; however, by that point, interest has cooled.

What changed between the beginning and end of this conversation was not the company, but how the stakeholders assessed risk based on it.

In today's world, lenders, investors, and regulators have encountered too many compelling stories that come apart.

They have come to believe that rapid growth can often mask weak foundations. Clean financial statements can conceal a lack of proper controls. Confident managers can disguise undisciplined decision-making. Because of this, the stakeholders are less afraid of slow growth than they are of hidden weaknesses.

The focus has changed; the evaluation is no longer only concerned with the numbers but also with how those numbers are produced, questioned, and governed. The stakeholders are now placing more value on behavior and decision-making processes than on forecasts; they are paying more attention to a company's internal discipline than to the stories being portrayed externally.

This is not a cynical response; it is a response based on experience.

Organizations that fail typically do so not because of a lack of ambition or opportunity. Instead, organizations typically fail because their internal level of discipline has not kept pace with their external growth. Specifically, the controls over cash have weakened; decisions are bypassed; and risk has accumulated slowly over time. The truth becomes evident through financial statements long after the organization has reached the point of no return.

External stakeholders have become aware of this problem and are now searching for signs of financial discipline within the organization's governance, culture, and day-to-day operations. Stakeholders want to see that their organization is growing with control, transparency, and accountability. To stakeholders, financial discipline will not be seen as a preference, but rather as a necessity.

The Great Shift in Stakeholder Expectations

Traditionally, stakeholder evaluation had a predictable pattern for decades. The lenders evaluated the company through the balance sheet and repayment ratios.

Investors evaluated the organization based on growth rates, margins, and projected future outlooks. Regulators evaluated the company for compliance with established rules. Snapshot assessments of evaluation performed reasonably well when the environment was steady, but when it was unstable, they continued to fail.

The issue was not that there was insufficient information. The issue was that stakeholders had an inflated perception of what the information actually represented.

Traditional practices for conducting due diligence have treated financial statements as objective truth, rather than curated outputs that have undergone the evaluation process. Stakeholders have assumed that the audited financial statements reflect the organization's proper "discipline". Consequently, over time, there have been numerous examples of organizations that were compliant but continued to operate dangerously. Controls were on paper, governance was in form, and discipline was displayed only when convenient.

Stakeholders began to recognize a pattern. Companies rarely fail suddenly. They deteriorated slowly. Minor exceptions became routine. Aggressive assumptions went unchallenged. Risks accumulated offstage while reported performance remained strong. By the time the damage surfaced in financial statements, capital was already impaired.

The cost of being fooled by managed numbers has been severe. Write-downs erased years of gains. Lenders absorbed losses that models never predicted. Regulators faced systemic fallout from firms that appeared healthy until they weren't. In every case, the issue was not the lack of data but the lack of behavioral insight.

A pattern began to emerge for stakeholders. Companies do not typically fail all at once; they slowly deteriorate.

Small exceptions eventually become commonplace. Bold assumptions go without being challenged. Offstage, the risks accumulate while the reported financial performance remains solid. By the time the financial statements reflect the damage, the capital has already been written down.

The financial industry has suffered substantial losses as a result of being deceived by numbers in managed financial statements. Write-downs wiped out years of gains. Financial institutions incurred losses that their models did not anticipate. Regulatory agencies have had to deal with systemic implications from companies that looked solid until they didn't. These situations demonstrate that the problem was not a lack of data, but rather a lack of insight into human behavior.

Today, lenders, investors, and regulators are less interested in isolated outcomes and more focused on organizational behavior. They are trying to understand whether discipline is embedded or improvised. The question is no longer just whether a company is performing, but whether it is designed to endure.

How Lenders See Financial Discipline Today

Financial discipline has a distinct meaning from a lender's lens; it's not about ambition or market share, nor is it about growth driven by headlines. Financial discipline through a lender's lens is based on predictability; lenders will be compensated to only focus on the downside risk, whereas upside stories won't get you paid.

For lenders, it isn't necessarily how fast your company is growing that matters most; rather, it's ensuring you'll be able to pay back the debt you have taken.

Financial discipline will become more important to lenders than your growth narrative, as lenders will view a fast-growing company with unreliable cash flow, no internal controls, and frequent covenant renegotiations as more hazardous than a steady-growing company with predictable cash generation and a disciplined approach to finances.

Lenders have determined that the faster a company grows, the more it will exhibit both positive and negative characteristics due to the amplifying effects of growth. There are many instances of companies that have grown rapidly but have also suffered significantly due to a lack of financial discipline; without discipline, rapid growth makes a company easily prone to instability.

Cash discipline is a key factor in how a lender evaluates a company. When lending, lenders will examine closely how a company monitors, protects, and deploys cash. They will also examine the company's balance sheet and cash flow statement, and look further into working capital management to identify timing mismatches between liabilities and the amount of cash available to support these liabilities. Companies that regularly stretch out their payment terms, rely on short-term loans to meet long-term obligations, or constantly refinance at the last minute provide lenders with an indication of undisciplined financial behavior.

How companies operate under their contractual obligations can help to provide additional evidence about a company. While lenders may not be overly concerned about the occasional violation, they would be more concerned about how a company handles it, including but not limited to promptly communicating the violation, providing reasonable and adequate explanations of the cause, and taking reasonable steps to remedy it. When a company provides all three of these elements, the lender builds more confidence in the company's ability to manage future problems. However, if a company repeatedly receives a covenant waiver from the lender, fails to communicate promptly about the waiver, or gives a creative reinterpretation of the terms, then the lender's confidence will erode significantly.

Therefore, how a company behaves when it violates its contractual obligations can indicate whether it has implemented meaningful corporate governance policies or exists to comply with rules.

How well a company has implemented its internal controls can significantly impact the lender's confidence that the information provided by the company can be relied upon. The reason for this is that when lenders evaluate a potential borrower, they want to know who makes decisions about large amounts of capital, how the company makes exceptions to its internal control processes, and whether the company is clear about decision-making authority during crises. When companies have weak internal controls, not only is the lender's operational risk significantly increased, but there is an even greater risk because of the uncertainty that can arise from the company's failure to maintain accurate reporting. Consequently, when a company violates its internal control processes, lenders have less visibility into its operations, which can lead to high costs due to uncertainty.

As a result, lenders prefer to work with what founders may call "boring" borrowers. Companies that provide transparent, conservative, and predictable reports and information will greatly reduce risk compared to those that offer aggressive growth plans. In this sense, "boring" can be defined as easily understood, governed, and relied upon by the lender.

The reason lenders have more difficulty sleeping when a company's margin is low is that they have no control over potential horrendous surprises.

Valuation to Governance

Investors were once rewarded for believing early and believing boldly. High valuations, aggressive projections, and rapid scaling were signals of opportunity rather than risk. That era has ended. Repeated losses have forced a recalibration. Today, many investors place far less trust in valuation than in governance.

Consistent with the traditional concept of value, Valuation can be easily manipulated by any party wishing to increase their perceived value. Even small changes in assumptions about growth rate, margin, and/or exit multiple can create large disparities in how investors value a company. Investors now know that a company's high Valuation does not always safeguard a company's capital. Instead, it can create a false sense of security and mask the risk being taken to justify the high Valuation. For this reason, many investors now view Culture/Ethics/Governance as the primary indicators of Long-Term Return on a Capital Investment. Culture/Ethics/Governance help determine how management responds to market changes. Culture/Ethics/Governance influence whether management reacts proactively or defensively under stress. Strong Governance does not prevent all mistakes, but it allows management to acknowledge them and correct them quickly (rather than ignoring or denying them).

Investors today generally see Profit as a trailing indicator of a company's performance. Profit is an indication of past decisions made by management. In the future, a company may generate profits from current trends or competitive advantages. Still, without Financial Discipline, those profits may lead to excessive confidence and risk-taking, thereby harming the company's long-term success. Conversely, Financial Discipline consistently builds and preserves value by limiting risk, maintaining optionality, and protecting Capital in an economic downturn.

With this change, there has been an increased separation between patient capital and momentum capital. Momentum capital focuses on rapid growth and a quick exit; it places less emphasis on sound discipline if the story is believable. In contrast, patient capital cares about predictability, governance quality, and internal resilience. In exchange for sacrificing short-term gains, patient capital investors seek the assurance of long-term viability and sustainability of their investment(s).

The most knowledgeable investors of the present day have shifted away from asking questions regarding the size of the market, but instead now ask about 'how' the company or firm makes decisions internally (allocation of capital, deliberation of risk, response to missing a target, etc.), indicating that the most knowledgeable investors are not looking for control of any sort over the companies they invest in, but rather, looking for trust.

Increasingly, investors are choosing discipline over flash, not because it is safer, but because it is ultimately more rewarding.

Systemic Discipline Over Reactive Compliance

The approaches regulators take to financial discipline differ in their underlying goals but are increasingly aligned with those of lenders and investors. Regulators do not seek growth or returns; instead, they work to maintain stability.

Over time, regulators have learned from experience that enforcement-based compliance is fragile. At the same time, compliance based upon discipline is far more enduring.

Compliance looks obviously different from compliance through enforcement; Compliance through disciplined organizations results in respect for the controls because of an understanding of their purpose.

The timeliness of reporting stems from it being an established, regular behavior, rather than a reaction to an impending deadline. Issues surrounding exceptions are raised earlier, in a climate of transparency, rather than addressed through reactive measures such as reminders, penalties, and notices of corrective actions. Compliance through reactive measures exists only while they are being overseen and will cease if the monitoring stops.

Organizations exhibiting systemic discipline will require far less regulatory intervention. Consistency in financial reporting, clear audit trails, and well-defined decision rights foster constructive regulatory engagement rather than adversarial. Issues can be resolved through dialogue rather than escalating to litigation. Enhanced data quality reduces the risk of misinterpretation, allowing for an earlier response.

This preference is not about being lenient; it is about creating efficiency and controlling risk. Regulators are responsible for monitoring very complex systems; thus, when a single organization fails, the ramifications can extend well beyond its financial records. Financially disciplined organizations provide a broader base of support for the system; they also reduce the likelihood of sudden failure, market disruption, and loss of public trust. From a regulatory perspective, stability is considered a public good. Stability protects employees, customers, other parties with whom an organization does business, and the overall economy.

Organizations that are committed to embedding financial discipline into their governance practices, their internal controls, and their culture will be perceived as lower-risk entities within the broader system. Therefore, these organizations tend to be more predictable, more transparent, and better able to respond to stress events.

As regulatory bodies continue to evolve their regulatory framework, the focus is now shifting from monitoring compliance with isolated compliance events to monitoring the ongoing maintenance and sustainability of financial discipline over time and through leadership succession. In this environment, organizations that operate as Financial Discipline Organizations do not just meet regulatory expectations. They align with the regulator's core objective: maintaining stability through disciplined design rather than reactive enforcement.

What Stakeholders Want to See in an FDO

Despite differences in approach to discipline among lenders, investors, & regulators, there are increasingly established similarities that create standard signals among them (mutual expectations). Stakeholders have become less confident in relying on the discipline of an organization based solely on assurances from lenders, investors, & regulators; they want to see how the organization is demonstrably exhibiting that discipline. The first of these signals is structured and audited reporting backing up the financial reporting structure. Stakeholders will look not only for accurate figures but also for traceable figures (audit trail). A stakeholder's confidence in financial reporting builds as the figures are produced accurately, showing that reporting has a direct link through the audit trail to transactions, approvals, and controls.

When financial reporting is consistent in timing and meaning and can be explained the same way regardless of who explains it, stakeholder confidence builds. If explanations change from one reporting cycle to the next, or vary by the person making the statement, stakeholder confidence erodes quickly.

Just as important to stakeholders is the visibility into cash flow; they are less focused on an organization's theoretical profits and more on liquidity resilience. They expect regular cash forecasting and cash budgeting to include realistic assumptions and to create cash reserves to absorb cash shocks. Proactive cash management will demonstrate an organization's ability to control cash. Any reliance on last-minute financing or emergency measures will indicate the organization's vulnerability. A third signal of a disciplined organization is internal narrative consistency, as opposed to external messaging. Stakeholders will watch closely to see if what an organization's leadership is telling its Board of Directors, employees, and investors is consistent. Any discrepancies among these statements will indicate confusion or concealment. In organizations with a disciplined operating culture, the discussion of brutal realities will take place internally before they become apparent externally; therefore, stakeholders will have minimal surprises because the information has been circulated openly. Accountability and escalation processes complete the full picture. Stakeholders want to know who is responsible for making financial decisions, how exceptions are handled, and when they need to escalate an issue. When the ownership of rights to consent is unclear to everyone, it adds risk. If everyone owns it, then no one owns it. A well-managed and controlled organization is clear about the ownership and allows escalation without fear.

The existence of these elements sets an FDO apart from a company with very high growth and very low discipline. A company with high growth was likely to have impressive reports at first, but a much worse audit trail. One moment, it may look like there was plenty of cash. The next moment, it turns out that there was not.

While cash was plentiful internally, the company had three hours of "optimistic" discussion before saying anything formally to the stockholders.

Accountability for decisions and risks surfaced early; decision explanations and conduct similar to various stakeholder audiences are not a certainty in a company that is not an FDO. What stakeholders want to see is not perfection but predictability. Not speed, but control over financial discipline, which the organization is also demonstrating through design vs. declaration.

How FDOs Reduce Stakeholder Risk

Financial discipline reduces risk not by eliminating uncertainty, but by making uncertainty manageable. For stakeholders, the value of an FDO lies in its behavior under changing conditions. Disciplined organizations do not promise stability. They deliver predictability.

One of the most significant and obvious benefits of using an FDO is that stakeholders receive fewer surprises. By identifying risk early, challenging assumptions, and surfacing deviations quickly, FDOs provide information flow so that stakeholders can respond rationally, rather than reacting to emotional responses from capital providers.

The second benefit is that organizations are better able to respond to crises faster. Disciplined organizations will have established frameworks, established escalation paths, and established data visibility before stress hits. Leaders do not waste time debating or seeking numbers; rather, they provide timely, well-coordinated action. This speed is the result of preparedness, not urgency. Stakeholders appreciate the reduced level of confidence lost due to delays rather than adversity.

Finally, the third benefit is a significant reduction in lost permanent capital. Capital losses will occur in every market cycle, and stakeholders wish to limit their exposure to irreparable damage arising from the denial of risk, the delay in action, or the uncontrolled accumulation of risk.

By establishing boundaries for risk and limiting downside exposure, FDOs minimize upside damage by allowing limited liquidity and eliminating the possibility of redeploying capital invested in losing assets. The result is that even where there are significant impairments of capital, a small percentage will be permanently lost.

Over time, these behaviors contribute to higher long-term portfolio performance. Organizations that protect downside while allowing measured upside compound value more reliably. Stakeholders may accept slower growth in exchange for durability. Returns generated with discipline tend to persist. Returns generated through excess tend to reverse.

Questions Stakeholders Should Be Asking

The key theme is that stakeholders' concern is not about news being negative. Stakeholders, including markets or lenders, can handle negative news. Their main concern is that the truth is not delivered promptly. Timely information about the truth supports the development of trust, offers options, and reduces extreme outcomes.

FDOs mitigate risk to the stakeholder by ensuring the truth is delivered early, clearly, and in a way that enables stakeholders to take action on it.

As the stakeholders' expectations change, so do the questions they will ask. Traditionally, stakeholders ask about projections, the available market, and financial ratios, all of which are important to consider; however, they do not provide the full picture. Therefore, in today's environment, it is important for stakeholders also to ask diagnostic questions that provide insight into the company's discipline in managing its financial resources, rather than simply looking at projected financial performance. Of these diagnostic questions, the one about how reporting integrity is maintained will provide the most insight into a company's overall financial discipline compared to any available projection of financial performance.

Stakeholders should ask not only whether reports are accurate but also how they ensure accuracy. They must be asked how they audit assumptions and handle exceptions. They must also be asked what happens when their actual performance does not match expectations. All of the answers to these questions indicate whether reporting is a disciplined process or managed; if it is managed, it means it was concluded outside a disciplined process that can provide credible reporting.

Another critical element of governance is decision-making. Many organizations feel uncomfortable when asked if any decisions were made without going through an approval process within the previous quarter. This discomfort is a good thing because it represents a healthy organization in which no single person can make significant decisions without input from others. In contrast, when a fragile organization encounters issues, it may rationalize poor decisions, justifying them by saying they were made in the best interests of the company or its stakeholders.

The information collected through variance analysis provides similar insight. For example, when stakeholders ask leadership which variance surprised them most and why, this provides an opportunity to evaluate the level of internal monitoring and transparency in discussions among members of the organization. Leadership in an FDO uses surprising variances to create opportunities for learning and improvement, while leadership in an undisciplined organization uses surprises to provide explanations after the fact.

Stakeholders should also explore how effectively the organization escalates or communicates "bad news." When was the last time a "bad news" scenario was escalated early? Who escalated the bad news? How did senior management respond to the escalated issue? The answers to these questions provide insight into whether the organization rewards or punishes transparency. Shifting the conversation from the organization's bottom line to its behavior provides valuable insight into the organization's level of discipline. In other words, stakeholders can determine whether the organization is disciplined under normal conditions, not just during crises. A projection of future results indicates what stakeholders hope will occur; diagnostic assessments of the organization provide insight into how the organization is currently operating. Numbers can be impressive. Answers are more complex to manage. This is why the right questions matter more than the most persuasive projections.

Cosmetic Compliance or True Financial Discipline

As financial discipline becomes a signal of credibility, many organizations respond by appearing disciplined rather than becoming disciplined. This creates a dangerous illusion.

Cosmetic compliance looks convincing in presentations and reviews, but it collapses under pressure. Superficial cost-cutting is a common example. Travel budgets are reduced, hiring freezes are announced, and minor expenses are scrutinized. At the same time, large capital decisions remain unchallenged. Acquisitions proceed without rigorous downside analysis. Long-term commitments are made based on optimistic assumptions. The message is inconsistent. Employees are asked to be frugal while leadership takes outsized risks. Stakeholders notice this gap quickly.

Frugality theatre often masks structural weaknesses. Saving on small operational costs creates the appearance of discipline, but it does nothing to correct flawed decision-making frameworks or weak governance. True discipline addresses how capital is allocated, not just how expenses are trimmed. It questions whether the organization is doing the right things, not just whether it is doing things cheaply.

Leadership signaling plays a decisive role. In cosmetically compliant organizations, discipline is enforced downward and exempt upward. Rules apply selectively. Exceptions are justified as strategic. Over time, this erodes credibility internally and externally. Stakeholders interpret selective discipline as risk tolerance without accountability.

True financial discipline looks different. It is consistent across levels. It applies to strategic decisions as rigorously as operational ones. It prioritizes clarity over comfort and governance over optics.

Cosmetic Compliance Versus Embedded Discipline		
Aspect	**Cosmetic Compliance**	**Embedded Discipline**
Cost Control	Focus on small expenses	Focus on capital allocation
Leadership Behavior	Rules apply selectively	Rules apply consistently
Decision Making	Driven by optics	Driven by risk-reward logic
Governance	Formal, reactive	Active, preventive
Stakeholder Trust	Short-term reassurance	Long-term confidence

Cosmetic compliance reassures in the short term but increases long-term risk. Embedded discipline may feel restrictive, but it builds resilience. Stakeholders are learning to distinguish between the two. Organizations that mistake appearance for substance eventually pay the price when scrutiny intensifies.

The FDO Advantage

Over time, financial discipline compounds in ways that are not immediately visible but deeply consequential. Organizations that operate as Financial Discipline Organizations become stakeholder-preferred not because they market themselves better, but because they behave more reliably. For lenders, this preference translates into improved credit terms. Predictable cash flows, transparent reporting, and disciplined covenant behavior reduce perceived risk. Lower risk earns better pricing, greater flexibility, and faster approvals. In periods of tightening liquidity, these advantages become decisive.

Investors respond in similar ways. Trust built through disciplined behavior leads to stronger investor loyalty.

Stakeholders who understand how decisions are made are less likely to exit at the first sign of volatility. They are more willing to support through downturns because they believe management will act responsibly. Over time, this trust lowers the cost of capital and attracts patient partners. Regulators also respond to discipline. Organizations that demonstrate consistent compliance, high- quality data, and proactive issue resolution experience fewer escalations and smoother interactions.

Regulatory goodwill is not favoritism. It is the natural outcome of reduced supervisory burden and lower systemic risk.

Perhaps most importantly, FDOs gain faster access to capital during crises. When markets tighten, stakeholders allocate capital toward organizations they trust to use it wisely. In those moments, reputational infrastructure matters more than reputation campaigns.

Being an FDO is not branding. It is infrastructure. It is built through consistent behavior, not declarations.

What Stakeholders Must Change Too

The shift toward financial discipline cannot rest solely on organizations. Stakeholders themselves must evolve. For years, lenders and investors rewarded speed, scale, and ambition, often at the expense of governance and control. This created incentives for indiscipline.

If discipline is to be sustained, stakeholders must stop rewarding speed over sustainability. Growth that outpaces control should be treated as a risk signal, not an achievement. Approval processes must incorporate measures of discipline alongside financial performance.

Building financial discipline metrics into approval and monitoring frameworks is essential.

Questions of governance quality, risk management, and decision-making should carry the same weight as projections and valuations. Monitoring should track consistency, not just outcomes.

Finally, stakeholders must learn to prefer survivability over upside-down fantasy. Long-term value is created by organizations that endure cycles, not by those that peak quickly and collapse. By aligning incentives with resilience, stakeholders reinforce the very discipline they seek.

This mutual shift is what will redefine trust in modern financial ecosystems.

The relationship between organizations and their stakeholders is undergoing a fundamental shift. Lenders, investors, and regulators are evolving faster than most companies realize. They are no longer satisfied with growth narratives, optimistic projections, or surface-level compliance. They are looking for evidence of discipline embedded in how organizations think, decide, and act.

In this environment, becoming a Financial Discipline Organization is no longer an internal aspiration. It is an external credibility signal. Across financial ecosystems, discipline has emerged as a proxy for trust. Organizations that demonstrate consistent governance, transparent reporting, and controlled decision-making are perceived as safer, more reliable, and more investable.

Financial discipline attracts patient, resilient capital. It draws stakeholders who value endurance over acceleration and predictability over spectacle. These stakeholders stay engaged during volatility, support corrective action, and contribute to long-term value creation. In contrast, organizations that rely on momentum and optics remain vulnerable to the sudden withdrawal of trust.

The implication is clear. Financial discipline is not defensive. It is strategic. It shapes who chooses to partner with you, fund you, and regulate you.

It determines whether scrutiny becomes an obstacle or a source of confidence.

The world is watching how disciplined your household is. But financial discipline is not just about surviving scrutiny. It is about building a legacy. The next chapter explores how FDO becomes a strategic moat that protects value long after leadership changes.

12

FDO AS A STRATEGIC MOAT

Two bridges exist in two separate cities. One is an iconic design. It has a contemporary appearance and is frequently photographed. It has design awards and praise from engineering sites for its beauty and use of new technology. The bridge was once proclaimed an engineering wonder; but then there was a winter season that wasn't expected, and the amount of weight it carried exceeded everyone's initial estimate and assumptions; plus there were shortcuts taken when maintaining the object; plus over time, many minor design flaws have continually compounded; therefore, this structure has not been values as gradually failing, but instead has failed due to some of these issues at once.

The second bridge is plain. It attracts no attention. It is rarely photographed and never celebrated. Its design is conservative. Its materials are reinforced. Its margins of safety appear excessive to those chasing efficiency. Decades pass. Traffic increases. Weather changes. The bridge remains.

Most organizations are constructed similarly in certain aspects.

Some organizations are affected by changes in their marketplaces, while others can no longer compete or have leadership.

What may now appear successful may be subject to future disadvantages.

Many businesses have structured themselves to capitalize on current trends; however, few have built a structure that will allow them to continue operating indefinitely.

Many of the things that create a business's competitive advantage can be measured easily.

Such things include brand identity, rapid growth, fair market value, market share, and speed of service.

Indeed, these things create the illusion of a strong company; however, as the income statement changes (or overall market conditions change), the competition disappears.

Discipline, however, is not as easily seen or measured.

Discipline does not have the same visibility as many of the visible competitive advantages.

Discipline is how businesses respond to various types of change, including declines in revenue, reductions in available capital for investment, and uncomfortable decision-making.

In the short term, markets reward a quick response; however, in the long term, markets reward disciplined management practices.

What Is a Strategic Moat and Why Most Are Temporary

"Moats" are about long-term survival, not market dominance or size... but about staying relevant in the future. A Strategic Moat is a structural "go-to-market advantage" that provides greater long-term value-creation protection against competition, volatility, and internal failure. While performance in a single calendar year may provide insight into how a moat has performed, durability over many cycles is a better indication of the moat's viability.

What Is a Strategic Moat?

A strategic moat is a structural advantage that protects long-term value creation by making failure, erosion, or displacement materially harder over time. Most organizations believe they have a moat. Many do not.

1. Product advantages get copied. Features that once differentiated become standard. Competitors catch up faster than expected.
2. Brand strength fades without consistent experience. Trust, once lost, is expensive to rebuild.
3. Cost leadership narrows as efficiency gains are replicated or offset by inflation, wage pressure, and complexity.
4. Even scale, often seen as the most vigorous defense, can become a liability when it creates rigidity instead of resilience.
5. The problem with most moats is that they are visible. Because they are visible, they are attacked. Because they are attacked, they erode.
6. Invisible moats behave differently.
7. They do not rely on secrecy or novelty.
8. They rely on behavior.
9. They are embedded in how decisions are made, how risks are evaluated, how capital is allocated, and how truth travels through the organization.

Financial discipline belongs to this category.

It does not prevent competition. It prevents collapse. It does not guarantee growth. It ensures survival with dignity and optionality. While others are forced into reactive decisions, disciplined organizations retain choice.

This is why financial discipline qualifies as a genuine strategic moat, even though it rarely appears on balance sheets or in investor presentations. It is not a control function. It is not the finance department's responsibility. It is an organizational capability that compounds quietly over time.

Why Financial Discipline Qualifies as a True Moat

Unlike many competitive advantages that are overtly announced, financial discipline is generally kept hidden. Operated behind the scenes, financial discipline impacts how decisions are framed within the organization, how risks are weighed against benefits, and how capital is treated. Financial discipline is not apparent in marketing campaigns or in quarterly reports. However, it is present in every significant organizational decision. This characteristic makes financial discipline an actual strategic moat.

Although it is difficult to identify a single example of financial discipline, it is present in almost every strategic move an organization makes and will impact how it grows; as long as it maintains its financial discipline, it will have a clear advantage in its marketplace. Furthermore, financial discipline is always present and dictates how an organization competes within its industry.

One way to understand this is to think of financial discipline as another competitor in the room. Not an external rival, but an internal force constantly testing decisions. When leaders ask, "What does discipline demand here?" They introduce friction that prevents reckless momentum. That friction is not a drag. It is protection.

What makes financial discipline uniquely powerful is that it is anti-fragile. Under stress, it does not weaken. It strengthens. Constraints become clearer. Priorities sharpen. Noise reduces.

While undisciplined organizations panic, disciplined ones become more deliberate.

This is where optionality matters. Financial discipline preserves choice. It allows leaders to delay, decline, pivot, or invest when others are forced to react. Forced decisions destroy value. Optional decisions create it.

Discipline also enables every other strategy. Innovation requires runway and tolerance for failure, both of which depend on cash clarity and risk boundaries. Acquisitions require restraint, valuation discipline, and patience in integration. Brand investment requires consistency and long-term funding. Talent retention depends on trust, stability, and credibility, especially during uncertainty.

None of these strategies survives without discipline underneath them.

Products compete. Marketing competes. Financial discipline endures.

Most moats erode when attacked. Financial discipline endures because it is not a target. It is a way of operating. It is measurable through behavior, durable across cycles, and transferable across leadership generations.

This is why organizations with embedded financial discipline often appear less dramatic in boom times, but far stronger when conditions turn. Their advantage compounds quietly, year after year, until it becomes undeniable.

How FDOs Withstand What Breaks Others

The real test of any strategic moat is not how it performs during expansion, but how it holds during stress. Financial Discipline Organizations reveal their advantage most clearly in moments that break others.

Undisciplined Organization Versus Financially Disciplined Organizations		
Context	**Undisciplined Org**	**FDO**
Downturns	Cash evaporates; reactive cuts	Buffers in place; controlled burn
Volatility	Emotional, ad-hoc decisions	Pre-set frameworks; clear accountability
Leadership Change	Discipline is tied to people	Discipline embedded in systems
Outcome	Value erosion	Resilient, ready to act

Discipline is codified, not improvised. Governance structures outlast individuals. Financial decision rules are understood across levels. Reporting integrity does not depend on who is in the room. As a result, succession does not trigger collapse. Continuity replaces chaos.

Five Things Only an FDO Can Withstand

1. A sudden funding freeze without panic
2. A prolonged downturn without cultural decay
3. Leadership transition without loss of control
4. Strategic pauses without loss of credibility
5. Growth opportunities without reckless overreach

This is the practical power of financial discipline as a moat. It does not eliminate risk. It absorbs shock. And in a volatile world, the ability to absorb shock is often the difference between survival and failure.

Financial Discipline and Long-Term Capital Outcomes

Many people think financial discipline is why businesses cannot grow quickly enough. However, financial discipline is one of the top indicators of a company's long-term success.

The key to understanding this difference is not speed, but rather how effectively the company can leverage its growth to create lasting value.

Organizations that use financial discipline have a different approach to capital allocation than do non- disciplined organizations. When looking for opportunities to grow, disciplined organizations do not jump on every opportunity that appears to provide growth potential. They focus on generating a return on investment rather than on excitement about growth, and on creating a long-term, sustainable business rather than a large organization.

Through disciplined use of capital, organizations will be able to utilize capital more effectively over time. Organizations that adopt a disciplined approach will avoid poor capital choices early in their evolution and provide appropriate support for good ones until those choices produce benefits.

One of the most evident effects is lower capital costs, as lenders and investors will offer better pricing based on greater predictability.

Organizations that consistently demonstrate cash discipline, conservative assumptions, and transparency in reporting will receive more favorable terms from lenders and investors than other organizations. Although this pricing advantage may seem negligible, over the long term, it produces a substantial competitive advantage. Margins of financial discipline also provide organizations with greater sustainability. Although disciplined organizations may not necessarily achieve better margin performance across all market cycles, they will be much more stable. Through disciplined pricing, controlled overhead costs, and realistic growth investment, disciplined organizations do not experience the margin volatility that many undisciplined organizations experience during economic downturns.

An increase in Return on Assets (ROA) can be attributed to a basic principle: something that you've invested in may be perceived as a resource that is NOT abundant. This means you'll need to intentionally control your inventory levels, debt levels, fixed asset levels, and labor force, thereby making your Working Capital management an advantage.

The most crucial distinction between organizations that have mastered Working Capital management and those that have not is the quality of their cash generation. Organizations with a disciplined approach to cash management not only monitor their cash earnings, but also continually monitor their Cash Flow.

Organizations that are disciplined in their cash management have established the importance of cash in terms of time, disclosures, and conversions; free cash flow provides a more reliable measure of performance than traditional accounting profit.

Across decades, this pattern repeats. Organizations that respect capital generate more of it. Those who misuse it eventually lose access.

Financial discipline does not cap growth. It shapes it. It ensures that growth strengthens the organization rather than hollowing it out from within.

FDO as a Reputation Engine

Many organizations view reputation as a communications issue when, in fact, it is an outcome of operations. The way an organization conducts its operations with Financial Discipline forms the basis for how it is viewed by all external stakeholders who depend on it.

For Investors, Financial Discipline is what creates the organization's credibility.

Charisma may create the initial entry into the conversation; however, consistency is what keeps the conversation open.

Disciplined organizations develop a reputation for realism.

The forecasts developed by disciplined organizations can be trusted because prior performance provides the foundation for them. Over time, these organizations will attract Patient Capital and not Speculative Momentum.

With Lenders, Financial Discipline creates a premium on predictability. Lenders have less uncertainty when they see transparent Cash Management, Covenant Compliance, and Early Communication of issues. Lenders are not concerned about modest performance; however, lenders do not want any surprises. Repeatedly demonstrating Financial Discipline allows organizations to earn flexibility with their lenders during times of greatest need.

Financial Discipline creates less friction with Regulators.

Regulatory Compliance becomes ingrained rather than an afterthought; therefore, Data Quality improves, Escalations decrease, and Building Trust develops silently over time. Trust does not eliminate Regulatory Scrutiny; however, it changes its nature from Suspicion to Supervision.

Organizations with Financial Discipline become the preferred partners in M&A transactions. Sellers trust disciplined organizations to close the deal, and counterparties trust the numbers they provide. Organizations with Financial Discipline will have a lower proportional risk of Integration as Governance and Controls mature. This created reputation serves to enhance the Strategic Options available to the disciplined organization. What makes this powerful is that it cannot be manufactured. You do not have market discipline.

You demonstrate it repeatedly. Quarter after quarter. Decision after decision. Crisis after crisis. Reputation built on discipline compounds. It attracts better stakeholders, better terms, and better opportunities.

And unlike branding campaigns, it does not decay when conditions change.

In the long run, discipline becomes the story others tell about you when you are not in the room.

Financial Discipline as a Legacy Builder

Most leaders think about performance in years. Financial Discipline Organizations think in decades.

Legacy is not created by peak performance. It is created by continuity. Organizations that survive leadership transitions, market cycles, and generational change do so because discipline outlives individuals. Financial discipline becomes the quiet mechanism through which values, judgment, and decision quality are transmitted over time.

This pattern is especially visible in multi-generational and family-owned enterprises that endure. Their advantage is rarely aggression or innovation alone. It is a restraint. Capital is treated as stewardship, not entitlement. Growth is pursued deliberately. Risk is understood not just in financial terms, but in reputational and cultural terms.

Culture plays a central role here. The disciplined organization's culture is not motivational language. It is a behavioral memory. People know how decisions are made, how trade-offs are evaluated, and how truth is handled. These habits persist even when leaders change. This is how financial discipline becomes cultural DNA.

Succession is where this matters most. Many organizations collapse not because the next leader is incompetent, but because the systems that supported judgment were never built.

Knowledge evaporates. Decision rights blur. Financial control weakens. What once worked intuitively stops working altogether.

Disciplined organizations preserve knowledge structurally. Decision frameworks are documented. Reporting integrity is protected. Governance does not depend on personalities.

As a result, new leaders inherit clarity rather than confusion.

Talent ecosystems form around such environments. High-quality professionals prefer organizations where decisions are rational, expectations are clear, and integrity is visible. Over time, this creates a reinforcing loop. Discipline attracts talent. Talent reinforces discipline.

This is the deeper value of financial discipline. It builds organizations that can survive their founders.

A useful question for any leader to ask is this: What will your organization retain after you are gone, habits or chaos?

Legacy is not what you build while you are present. It is what continues to work when you are not.

The Hidden Risk of Founder-Centric Intuition

Founder intuition is powerful. It enables speed, conviction, and early momentum. Many organizations would not exist without it. The risk begins when intuition becomes the primary operating system.

Founder-centric organizations often appear strong while the founder is present. Decisions are fast. Authority is clear. Financial judgment is centralized. Over time, however, this creates a fragile dependency. Discipline lives in the person, not the organization.

When founders step back, sell, or lose influence, the consequences surface quickly. Control collapses. Strategic direction fragments. Teams hesitate. Financial decisions stall or conflict.

What was once clarity becomes paralysis.

Often, boards do not value the transition risk as they see founder experience as naturally transferable. This is very rarely true, as most of the time, intuition is not based on any form of structure and therefore does not scale. Intuition, lacking structure, cannot be consistently taught, audited, or reproduced under stress.

Culturally, founder-centric models create "silos" of information. Rather than enabling accountability, loyalty is the primary motivating factor for many of the people involved. Questioning behavior is generally discouraged. Founder confidence overshadows financial caution. As a result, when the founder leaves the organization, it will most likely fracture because the underlying culture was never institutionalized.

The financial impact is dramatic due to incoherence in capital allocation. Additionally, there is a significant increase in risk exposure without anyone realizing it. Reporting is mainly cosmetic. Strategically, the organization believes it is stable, yet drifts away from its intended purpose.

Financial discipline will mitigate these issues. Financial discipline does not replace leadership vision. Financial discipline supports leadership vision. Financial discipline converts an individual leader's subjective judgment into an organization's objective capability and ensures that quality decision- making endures through inevitable transitions.

Financial discipline scales continuity. Founder intuition can create a lasting impact. Financial discipline will enable organizations that realize the importance of this to transition from becoming a "heroic dependency" to an "institutional strength". These organizations develop systems that honor the founder's intuition, while also creating a more systematic basis of documentation.

This transition is the primary difference between a "great founder story" and an "enduring institution.

The FDO World: When Financial Discipline Becomes Universal.

This section is a forward-looking assumption, not a prediction. It explores what the business world could look like if financial discipline at the level of a Financial Discipline Organization (FDO) were widely adopted across firms, institutions, and markets.

The intention is not to claim certainty, but to examine direction. Short-term decisions, volatility, and reactive behavior often shape today's business environment. The FDO framework offers an alternative path, one where disciplined decision-making, structured governance, and aligned systems create greater consistency and resilience.

By imagining a shift from the present state to an FDO-driven world, we can better understand the potential impact of financial discipline at scale. Such a transition would not eliminate uncertainty, but it could make business outcomes more predictable, decisions more accurate, and the broader economic system more stable and trustworthy.

What follows is an exploration of that possibility.

The Year is 2035: Welcome to the FDO Economy

1. Global FDO Adoption: 94%
2. Market Efficiency: 89%
3. Value Creation Rate: 47% CAGR
4. Economic Waste: <3%
5. Business Failure Rate: 2.1%

The Transformation is complete. Here's how the world changed...

I. THE GREAT REWIRING: How Everything Connected

The Universal Language Emerged

PRESENT WORLD (2026)

- Company A: "We're growing fast!"
- Company B: "We're innovative!"
- Company C: "We're customer-focused!"
- Result: ??? (No common measurement)

FDO WORLD (2036)

- Company A: "ROIC 34%, targeting 40%."
- Company B: "Innovation ROI: 8.2x"
- Company C: "Customer LTV/CAC: 12:1"
- Result: Instant understanding, comparison, collaboration

The Network Effect

When everyone speaks, Financial Discipline:

1. Partnerships form in minutes, not months
2. Due diligence takes hours, not weeks
3. Integration happens seamlessly
4. Value chains optimize automatically

Real Example:

- Monday 9 AM: Companies identify synergy
- Monday 2 PM: Models merged, ROI calculated
- Tuesday 10 AM: Partnership lives
- Wednesday: First value created
- Old World Timeline: 6-12 months

II. THE BANKING REVOLUTION: From Lending to Value Partnership

Financial Institutions in 2026 (Pre-FDO World)

Function	Reality	Problem
Risk Assessment	Historical financials	Backward-locking
Lending Decision	Collateral-based	Misses' potential
Relationship	Transactional	No real partnership
Value Add	Capital only	Limited impact
Default Rate	3-5%	Massive waste

Financial Institutions in 2036 (FDO World)

Function	Reality	Result
Risk Assessment	Real-time value metrics	Future-focused
Lending Decision	ROI-model-based	Funds winners
Relationship	Value co-creation	True partnership
Value Add	Capital + optimization	Multiplied returns
Default Rate	0.3%	Near-zero waste

The New Banking Model

"Value Creation Banks" (VCBs):

Traditional Loan: Here's $10M at 8%

VCB Partnership: Here's $10M + our AI will help you to increase your ROIC by 12%

Your success = Our success

Banking Career Evolution:

1. 2026: "Relationship Manager."
2. 2036: "Value Creation Partner."
3. Salary difference: 5x

Radical Innovations in Banking

Instant Capital Allocation

1. Company uploads real-time metrics
2. AI analyzes value creation potential
3. Capital approved in seconds
4. Terms adjust dynamically with performance

Reverse Banking

1. Banks pitch companies they want to fund
2. Based on value creation algorithms
3. "Your metrics show you should expand to Brazil."
4. "Here's $50M pre-approved for 31% ROI"

Risk Elimination Through Transparency

Every company shares:

1. Real-time P&L
2. Live cash position
3. Forward projections
4. Value creation metrics

Result: Banks prevent problems before they happen

III. THE INVESTOR TRANSFORMATION: From Assumption to Science

Venture Capital in FDO World

PRESENT VC Model (2026):

100 investments → 90 fail → 9 return capital → 1 unicorn

Success Rate: 1%

Waste: $Billions

FDO VC Model (2036):

100 investments → 5 fail → 85 return 3-5x → 10 return 20x+

Success Rate: 95%

Waste: Minimal

Why the Dramatic Shift?

1. Every startup born with FDO DNA
2. Unit economics are clear from day 1
3. Scaling models proven before funding
4. Pivot decisions data-driven, fast

Public Markets Revolution

Stock Price Determination:

1. 2026: Sentiment + Story + Momentum
2. 2036: Value Creation Rate × Sustainability Score × Innovation ROI

Results:

1. Market volatility: -87%
2. Valuation accuracy: +94%
3. Insider trading: Impossible (everything's transparent)
4. Market crashes: Extinct

New Investment Vehicles

1. **Value Creation Funds (VCFs)**
    1. Invest only in the top 10% FDO performers
    2. Returns: 34% annually, low volatility
    3. Accessible to everyone via tokenization
2. **ROI Prediction Markets**
    1. Bet on companies hitting ROI targets
    2. Creates additional accountability
    3. Rewards accurate analysis
3. **Discipline Score Derivatives**
    1. Trade based on FDO execution
    2. Hedge against discipline degradation
    3. Price discipline in the market

IV. STRATEGIC PARTNERSHIPS: From Politics to Mathematics

Partnership Formation in FDO World

The Present Way (2026):

- Months 1-3: Getting to know each other
- Months 4-6: Exploring synergies
- Months 7-9: Negotiating terms
- Months 10-12: Lawyers fighting
- Months 13+: Maybe launching
- Success Rate: 20%

The FDO Way (2036):

- Hour 1: Exchange value creation models
- Hour 2: AI calculates optimal structure
- Hour 3: Smart contract created
- Hour 4: Partnership lives
- Success Rate: 89%

Revolutionary Partnership Models

1. **Value Fusion Networks**

Company A (ROIC 30%) + Company B (ROIC 35%) = Fusion Entity (ROIC 55%)

Automatic value sharing based on contribution

No politics, only mathematics

2. **Skill Arbitrage Platforms**
    1. Company A: "We have excess AI capability."
    2. Company B: "We need AI, have distribution."
    3. Platform: Calculates optimal exchange
    4. Value created: Split automatically
3. **Temporary Value Alliances**
    1. Form for a specific opportunity
    2. Dissolve when ROI is achieved

3. No emotional baggage
4. Pure value creation

The End of Corporate Politics

What Disappeared:

1. Ego-driven partnerships
2. Relationship-based deals
3. Political alliances
4. Hidden agendas

What Emerged:

1. Data-driven combinations
2. Value-optimized structures
3. Transparent governance
4. Aligned incentives

V. THE ECONOMIC TRANSFORMATION: Efficiency Unprecedented

Macro-Economic Metrics

Indicator	2026	2036 (FDO)	Impact
Global GDP Growth	3.1%	12.4%	4x acceleration
Resource Efficiency	100	340	3.4x improvement
Business Failure Rate	21%	2.1%	10x reduction
Innovation Success	11%	73%	7x improvement
Capital Allocation Efficiency	100	890	8.9x better
Economic Cycles	±15%	±2%	Stability achieved

New Economic Phenomena

1. **The Great Convergence**
    1. Developing economies caught up in 5 years

2. Why? FDO doesn't require infrastructure
3. Just discipline and data
4. Global inequality: -73%

2. **Productivity Explosion**

   Average Worker Output:

   2026: $150k/year

   2036: $1.2M/year How?

   Every decision optimized for value

3. **The Waste Elimination**
   1. Zombie companies: Extinct
   2. Vanity projects: Impossible
   3. Corporate welfare: Ended
   4. Result: $47T redirected to value creation

Government Transformation

FDO Governments:

1. Every program has ROI metrics
2. Real-time citizen dashboards
3. Automatic funding adjustment
4. Political promises require models

Results:

1. Government efficiency: +400%
2. Citizen satisfaction: 89%
3. Corruption: Near zero (can't hide numbers)
4. Public debt: Decreasing globally

VI.PAIN POINTS ELIMINATED: The Problems That No Longer Exist

1. Information Asymmetry → Extinct

Present World: Insiders win, outsiders lose

FDO World: Everyone sees everything, markets perfect

2. Capital Misallocation → Solved

Present World: Money flows to the best storytellers

FDO World: Money flows to value creators automatically

3. Business Cycles → Smoothed

Present World: Boom/bust is inevitable

FDO World: Continuous optimization, micro-adjustments

4. Startup Mortality → Minimized

Present World: 90% fail in 5 years

FDO World: 90% succeed (pivot fast with data)

5. Corporate Fraud → Impossible

Present World: Hidden until the explosion

FDO World: Real-time transparency, instant detection

6. Wage Stagnation → Reversed

Present World: Value creation unclear, wages flat

FDO World: Value measured precisely, shared fairly

7. Innovation Waste → Eliminated

Present World: Billions on failed R&D

FDO World: Kill bad ideas in days, not years

8. M&A Failures → Rare

Present World: 70% destroy value

FDO World: 94% create value (math, not ego)

9. Market Manipulation → Ended

Present World: Pump and dump, false signals

FDO World: Only fundamentals matter

10. Economic Anxiety → Gone

Present World: Uncertainty everywhere

FDO World: Predictable value creation

VII. THE SOCIAL TRANSFORMATION: How We Live Differently

Career Paths Revolutionized

2026 Career: Climb ladder slowly, politics matter

2036 Career: Create value, advance immediately

New Reality:

1. 22-year-old with proven ROI → CEO
2. 50-year-old without discipline → Unemployable
3. Merit purely mathematical

Education Transformed

Elementary School:

1. Basic ROI concepts
2. Value creation games
3. Financial discipline as a life skill

Universities:

1. Every major includes FDO
2. Thesis = Business case
3. Graduation = Value proven

Personal Relationships

Dating Apps 2036:

1. Financial discipline scores are visible
2. Value creation potential matched
3. Shared ROI goals

Marriage Success Rate:

1. 2026: 80%
2. 2036: 95%
3. Why? Aligned on value, clear on goals

VIII. TECHNOLOGICAL ENABLERS: The FDO Tech Stack

Universal Value API

1. Every company is connected
2. Real-time value exchange
3. Automatic optimization
4. Zero integration cost

AI Value Maximizers

1. Continuously optimize operations
2. Suggest partnership opportunities
3. Predict value creation paths
4. Eliminate human bias

Blockchain Value Ledgers

1. Every value creation recorded
2. Immutable ROI history
3. Automatic value distribution
4. Trust through transparency

Quantum ROI Modeling

1. Calculate infinite scenarios
2. Find optimal paths instantly
3. Predict 20+ years out
4. Uncertainty eliminated

IX. THE FUTURE BEYOND 2035

2040: Interplanetary FDO

1. Mars colony ROI positive
2. Space resources allocated efficiently
3. No waste in space

2045: Post-Scarcity Achievement

1. FDO efficiency = Abundance

2. Work becomes optional
3. Value creation for joy

2050: The Final Evolution

1. Human consciousness merged with FDO
2. Think in value creation naturally
3. Species-level optimization

X. THE PHILOSOPHICAL IMPLICATIONS

What We Gained:

1. Clarity of purpose
2. Fairness in outcomes
3. Sustainable prosperity
4. Measurable meaning
5. Collective optimization

What We Lost:

1. Comfortable delusions
2. Political manipulation
3. Wasteful romanticism
4. Inequality systems
5. Boom/bust drama

The Net Result:

Humanity upgraded from Homo Economicus to Homo Disciplines

The Call to Action

You're living in a transitional moment.

Every company that adopts FDO now becomes a founding member of the new world. Every leader who embodies FDO now becomes an architect of the future.

The question isn't whether this world will emerge—it's whether you'll help create it or be consumed by it.

Your Next Steps:

1. **Tomorrow:** Start your FDO transformation
2. **Next Month:** Show first results
3. **Next Quarter:** Become a case study
4. **Next Year:** Lead the revolution
5. **Next Decade:** Shape the new world

The FDO World isn't a prediction—it's an inevitability.

The only variable is timing.

And timing, in this case, is everything.

Because the companies starting today won't just survive the transition—they'll own the future.

Welcome to the FDO Revolution. Your transformation begins now.

What a World of FDOs Looks Like

When financial discipline becomes pervasive within an organization, it affects how other organizations interact with it. Financial discipline organizations enable fast transactions because trust no longer needs to be established as a precondition. The time each counterparty spends verifying, renegotiating, or hedging against a partner engaging in destructive behavior is significantly reduced. As a result, contracts are simpler, and credit decisions are made much faster. As a result, capital flows with greater confidence, as the likelihood of hidden surprises is lower. Wasted resources through the system are reduced. Resources are allocated with purpose vs inertia, so fewer projects are left incomplete, fewer acquisitions are subsequently written down, and fewer restructurings are done to reverse excesses that could have been avoided.

The cost of failure has not been eliminated, but the frequency of preventable failures is far lower.

The capital efficiency of the entire financial system improves. The productive use of money lasts longer, and returns become significantly more predictable. Long-term investing becomes more attractive than speculative behavior; however, that shift does not stifle innovation; rather, it enhances the quality of innovation by matching ambition with accountability. The behavioral patterns of today's markets are rapidly changing. Valuations are now based less on optimistically crafted narratives and more on the company's credibility from a commercial perspective.

Instead of simply viewing "growth" as a measure of success, measuring growth must also include resilience.

Furthermore, the success of a business will no longer be judged by its size; instead, it will be evaluated based on whether it can survive over time.

The effects of financial discipline at the societal level extend beyond infrastructure. Similar to how we don't notice the impact of infrastructure (e.g., roads, power grids, etc.) unless it's there, we will notice the absence of infrastructure when it's lacking, creating ripples through society. When infrastructure fails, the result is job loss, erosion of trust, and public confidence.

Financial Discipline Organizations (FDOs) help mitigate those effects. They do not eliminate risk; they provide a way to contain the risk. By containing risk, FDOs stop localized failures from becoming system-wide crises and the long-term evolution of healthier financial systems and stronger economic participation.

This vision is not a pipe dream; it's pragmatic. It doesn't require perfect behavior, only routine discipline and incremental improvement starting from one organization.

Those organizations can choose to design their business rather than improvise.

FDOs are not finance upgrades. They are strategic moats that protect a company's value during times of distress and compound that advantage during times of prosperity. Organizations that create and embed financial discipline can fail; however, because they have created structures around financial discipline, they will fail less frequently. They will protect the organization's trust, capital, and optionality through all economic cycles.

Most importantly, they build something that survives leadership changes. Legacy is not built through slogans or vision statements. It is built through habits that endure when the spotlight moves on.

Growth impresses. Discipline endures.

And in a volatile world, endurance is the rarest advantage of all.

CONCLUSION

The underlying concept of this book has always been that financial discipline is not simply about saving; rather, it is about being financially responsible, planning well into the future, and having a plan to achieve your organization's financial goals. Organizations, as a rule, do not set out with the intention of being financially undisciplined. Financial indiscipline develops as a result of excessive growth, lack of trust, and confusion between the real and perceived success of the organization, creating a gap between accountability and decision-making, what is reported and the actual state of affairs, and between the authority to make decisions and the responsibility to carry out the decisions made.

A Financial Discipline Organization (FDO) will experience failure like any other organization. An FDO recognizes and responds to risk more quickly and has a greater capacity to recover from that risk than a non-FDO organization. It does not rely on individual heroics, market fortune, or continuous growth; rather, it relies on a structured, well-defined culture and consistent behavioral methods.

What makes an FDO an FDO is not perfection, but predictability; it is not rigidity, but clarity, and it does not require control. An FDO ensures alignment among risk, reward, and accountability, rather than control for its own sake.

Financial discipline changes how leaders lead an organization.

Financial discipline creates opportunities for uncomfortable conversations and decision-making well in advance of crises, shifts the locus of decision-making from the leader's personality to a systematic set of processes, and places greater emphasis on evidence rather than instinct. Over time, financial discipline will change the organization's culture. Employees will learn that truth comes before optimism; stakeholders will learn that transparency is unconditional. Decision-making in the organization will improve as incentives align with long-term outcomes.

A key principle of financial discipline is its long-term nature. An organization's financial strategies may vary from leader to leader. Markets and business conditions will continue to change. However, an organization with financial discipline embedded in its culture and governance will pass it on generation after generation. Therefore, success will become part of a legacy. Thus, the financial discipline discussed in this book offers ambitious leaders an opportunity to create a legacy of leadership.

This book does not suggest that leaders should choose a conservative leadership approach over a bold or ambitious one; instead, it shows how bold and ambitious leaders can build a solid leadership legacy through financial discipline. Therefore, financial discipline represents the highest level of leadership.

The organizations that truly understand the importance of financial discipline to a leader's ability to build a legacy will not be the most visible leaders in the marketplace. Instead, they will still exist after all other organizations in the marketplace have disappeared.

ABOUT THE AUTHOR

Venkatesh KAP is a distinguished senior executive in the banking industry with nearly two decades of expertise in loan portfolio management. Throughout his career, he has successfully managed substantial credit portfolios across diverse industry sectors, including the strategic turnaround of distressed assets. His extensive experience with defaulted companies revealed a critical pattern: the primary catalyst for organizational failure is financial indiscipline.

This pivotal insight drives Venkatesh's mission to raise awareness about the paramount importance of financial discipline in organizational sustainability. His vision is uncompromising: to build resilient organizations through financial discipline, ensuring that no organization worldwide falls victim to financial mismanagement.

As Founder and Chief Executive Officer of Ebitaus, a pioneering fintech organization, Venkatesh delivers innovative solutions to financial institutions and their corporate clients. He partners strategically with client leadership teams to transform organizational strategy into structured, actionable implementations. Through robust systems, sophisticated tools, and comprehensive governance frameworks, he provides organizations with clear compliance enhancement and sustainable operational excellence.

Before establishing Ebitaus, Venkatesh held senior positions at premier financial institutions, where he honed his expertise in credit management and organizational financial health.

Throughout his distinguished career, Venkatesh has remained focused on one fundamental question: How can organizations develop enduring financial strength that transcends short-term performance metrics? He firmly believes that organizational effectiveness is achieved through the strategic integration of well-structured technology systems, consistent flows of reliable information, and robust decision-making frameworks—forming the cornerstone for sustained performance amid growth and market uncertainty.

DISCLAIMER

This book is intended solely for educational, informational, and conceptual understanding purposes. The content has been prepared with the intention of explaining the subject matter clearly and effectively for readers.

The author and publisher have made reasonable efforts to ensure that the information, data, facts, statistics, references, and examples included in this book are accurate and up to date at the time of publication. Such information has been compiled and referred from multiple publicly available sources, industry references, and other secondary materials believed to be reliable.

However, despite due care and diligence, inadvertent errors, omissions, interpretational differences, or changes in facts, laws, regulations, policies, or market conditions may occur over time. The author and publisher do not warrant the absolute accuracy, completeness, or continued validity of such information.

Readers are advised to independently verify critical facts, legal positions, financial data, regulatory requirements, and professional matters before relying upon them for decision-making, compliance, business, legal, financial, or other professional purposes.

The views, interpretations, and explanations presented in this book are those of the author for educational purposes and should not be construed as legal, financial, regulatory, tax, compliance, or professional advice.

Neither the author nor the publisher shall be held liable for any direct, indirect, incidental, consequential, or incidental loss, damage, claim, or liability arising from the use of, reliance upon, or interpretation of the contents of this book.

If any factual inaccuracies or discrepancies are identified, they are entirely unintentional, and the author requests readers' understanding in such instances.

Source Compilation Disclaimer

The company-specific information, business details, operational references, financial data, case studies, and related descriptions presented in this book have been compiled, analyzed, and consolidated from multiple publicly available sources and are not derived from or attributable to any single specific source, organization, publication, or institution.

These sources may include company websites, public disclosures, regulatory filings, annual reports, industry publications, market reports, news articles, research papers, and other publicly accessible materials considered relevant and reliable at the time of writing.

The purpose of such compilation is solely to provide broader conceptual understanding, comparative analysis, and educational insight for readers. The author does not represent any single source as the exclusive basis of such information and does not imply official endorsement, validation, or authorization by any particular company or institution.

Accordingly, the author shall not be held responsible for variations, inconsistencies, interpretational differences, or subsequent updates arising from the use of information compiled across multiple independent sources.

www.ingramcontent.com/pod-product-compliance
Lightning Source LLC
LaVergne TN
LVHW101443200926
848483LV00001B/31